Ali Baba and the Forty Thieves

A pantomime

Norman Robbins

Samuel French - London
New York - Toronto - Hollywood

© 1991 BY NORMAN ROBBINS

Rights of Performance by Amateurs are controlled by Samuel French Ltd, 52 Fitzroy Street, London W1P 6JR, and they, or their authorized agents, issue licences to amateurs on payment of a fee. **It is an infringement of the Copyright to give any performance or public reading of the play before the fee has been paid and the licence issued.**

The Royalty Fee indicated below is subject to contract and subject to variation at the sole discretion of Samuel French Ltd.

Basic fee for each and every
performance by amateurs   Code L
in the British Isles

The Professional Rights in this play are controlled by SAMUEL FRENCH LTD, 52 FITZROY STREET, LONDON W1P 6JR.

The publication of this play does not imply that it is necessarily available for performance by amateurs or professionals, either in the British Isles or Overseas. Amateurs and professionals considering a production are strongly advised in their own interests to apply to appropriate agents for consent before starting rehearsals or booking a theatre or hall.

ISBN 0 573 06485 7

Please see page iv for further copyright information.

CHARACTERS

Tinbad, a poor tailor
Cascara, Ali Baba's housekeeper
Ali Baba, a poor woodcutter
Haroun, his son
Marsaina, a slave-girl
Morgana, Mistress of Fates
Avarice, an evil Afrit
Kassim Baba, Ali's rich, miserly brother
Rhum Baba, his snooty wife
Hanki Panki, a failed thief
Jiggeri Pokeri, his companion
Al Raschid, ruthless leader of The Forty Thieves
Achmed the 'Orrible, one of his men

Chorus of **Citizens, Merchants, Slaves, Thieves, Dancing Girls, Babes,** etc.

COPYRIGHT INFORMATION

(See also page ii)

This play is fully protected under the Copyright Laws of the British Commonwealth of Nations, the United States of America and all countries of the Berne and Universal Copyright Conventions.

All rights, including Stage, Motion Picture, Radio, Television, Public Reading, and Translation into Foreign Languages, are strictly reserved.

No part of this publication may lawfully be reproduced in ANY form or by any means—photocopying, typescript, recording (including video-recording), manuscript, electronic, mechanical, or otherwise—or be transmitted or stored in a retrieval system, without prior permission.

Licences for amateur performances are issued subject to the understanding that it shall be made clear in all advertising matter that the audience will witness an amateur performance; that the names of the authors of the plays shall be included on all announcements and on all programmes; and that the integrity of the authors' work will be preserved.

The Royalty Fee is subject to contract and subject to variation at the sole discretion of Samuel French Ltd.

In Theatres or Halls **seat**ing Four **Hundred** or more the fee will be subject to negotiation.

In Territories Overseas the fee quoted in this Acting Edition may not apply. A fee will be quoted on application to our local authorized agent, or if there is no such agent, on application to Samuel French Ltd, London.

VIDEO RECORDING OF AMATEUR PRODUCTIONS

Please note that the copyright laws governing video-recording are extremely complex and that it should not be assumed that any play may be video-recorded *for whatever purpose* without first obtaining the permission of the appropriate agents. The fact that a play is published by Samuel French Ltd does not indicate that video rights are available or that Samuel French Ltd controls such rights.

A licence issued by Samuel French Ltd to perform this play does NOT include permission to use any copyright music in the performance. The notice printed below on behalf of the Performing Right Society should be carefully read.

The following statement concerning the use of music is printed here on behalf of the Performing Right Society Ltd, by whom it was supplied

The permission of the owner of the performing right in copyright music must be obtained before any public performance may be given, whether in conjunction with a play or sketch or otherwise, and this permission is just as necessary for amateur performances as for professional. The majority of copyright musical works (other than oratorios, musical plays and similar dramatico-musical works) are controlled in the British Commonwealth by the PERFORMING RIGHT SOCIETY LTD, 29–33 BERNERS STREET, LONDON W1P 4AA.

The Society's practice is to issue licences authorizing the use of its repertoire to the proprietors of premises at which music is publicly performed, or, alternatively, to the organizers of musical entertainments, but the Society does not require payment of fees by performers as such. Producers or promoters of plays, sketches, etc., at which music is to be performed, during or after the play or sketch, should ascertain whether the premises at which their performances are to be given are covered by a licence issued by the Society, and if they are not, should make application to the Society for particulars as to the fee payable.

SYNOPSIS OF SCENES

ACT I
Scene 1 The Great Market-Place in Cairo
Scene 2 The Oasis of the Seven Palms
Scene 3 Outside the Magic Cave
Scene 4 A quiet street
Scene 5 Outside Ali Baba's house

ACT II
Scene 1 The Market-Place again
Scene 2 The Street of Lesser Merchants
Scene 3 The Market-Place once more
Scene 4 A quiet street
Scene 5 The Banqueting Hall of Ali's new house
Scene 6 A corridor
Scene 7 The Banqueting Hall and Finale

AUTHOR'S NOTE

Ali Baba was the first pantomime I ever appeared in, and even forty-odd years ago productions of this particular subject were few and far between. I always considered this strange, as the colourful costumes and opportunities for spectacle were just as great as for *Aladdin*, a far more popular pantomime.

One of the problems, I could see clearly: the Forty Thieves themselves. Few professional managements could have forty brawny men in the chorus, and certainly no group of amateurs I knew boasted such talent. The obvious solution, then, was to reduce the numbers by always having some of them off-stage. This is what I've done with this version. The Forty Thieves of course, though always assumed to be men, could well include ladies made-up and dressed in appropriate manner.

A second problem was that Ali Baba is probably one of the most blood-thirsty tales of the Arabian Nights stories. A quick scan through the original would make one's flesh creep. Judicious editing, I hope, has removed most of the horrors, with just enough left to add menace to this ... one of the most exciting tales to come from the East, and for all intents and purposes, one of the first detective stories. (Note how Raschid almost tracks down Ali Baba, only to be foiled by Marsaina.)

The third problem was that Ali Baba was not really a pantomime at all. There was no Fairy and Demon element, and no Dame and Simple Simon character. These I have added. I hope purists will forgive me.

The occupation of Tinbad, who in the original story was a cobbler, I have changed to a tailor. This I feel is more real to the children of today who would not associate a cobbler with sewing.

Songs should reflect, as far as possible, an eastern "feel" and obviously the more colourful the costumes and scenery are, the better. There is no need for masses of messy body make-up, and dancing girls should be bare-footed. The rest of the characters should wear eastern-type slippers, or at least "flatties". Keep the lighting warm but apart from that, you have here a truly traditional pantomime which should delight your patrons for a long time to come.

Best of Luck

Norman Robbins

For

John Richardson

who, after a long and distinguished career in the professional theatre, was introduced to me and in the space of a few short years found himself playing amongst other things, my brother in a straight play, my ugly sister in pantomime, my partner in a radio documentary, my director in a World Première, and my straight man in countless "Entertainments". This'll teach you not to go "slumming".

Other plays by Norman Robbins published by Samuel French Ltd:

Aladdin
Cinderella
Dick Whittington
Grand Old Duke of York
Hickory Dickory Dock
Humpty Dumpty
Late Mrs Early
Nightmare
Pull The Other One
Rumpelstiltzkin
Sing A Song of Sixpence
Slaughterhouse
Sleeping Beauty
Tom, the Piper's Son
Tomb With A View
Wedding of the Year
Wonderful Story of Mother Goose

ACT I

Scene 1

The Great Market-Place in Cairo

An eastern market-place with a backdrop of stylized minarets, stalls, palms, etc. The area is packed with merchants and customers, bargaining or in search of a bargain. Slave girls are dancing in colourful costumes in front of one of the booths, and trinket sellers wander through the throng. To the delight of children, a snake charmer sits on a mat playing his pipe whilst a snake wavers gently from inside a woven basket. Eastern type music plays insistently and the whole picture should be one of colour, movement, noise and great heat. As the full effect is realised by the audience, the first of the sellers begins to call his (or her) wares. The cry is taken up by others and this leads into a full throated rendering of the Opening Chorus

Song 1 (Choristers)

At the end of the song, Tinbad the tailor hurries on UR. *He is shabbily but garishly dressed in turban, silk blouse and baggy pants, and carries a sheet of paper, which he waves excitedly. He moves quickly* DC

Tinbad (*breathlessly*) Oooh. Hey. Listen everybody. Listen. I'm going to be rich. I'm going to have so much money I won't know what to do with it. Isn't it *smashing*?
Merchant 1 (*stepping forward*) My dear friend Tinbad, calm yourself. There's no need to get so excited. Surely you've had letters from the Reader's Digest before?
Tinbad No, no. I'm not talking about *them*. It's this. (*He shows the paper*) I copied it down from the city notice-board a few minutes ago. Look. (*He hands it to the Merchant*)
Merchant 1 (*reading it aloud*) By order of His Highness, the Calif of Cairo, a reward of ten thousand dinars shall be given to anyone who can lead the Royal Army to the hiding place of Al Raschid and his villainous Forty Thieves.

There is a general reaction

Tinbad (*eagerly*) You see? You see? All I've got to do is find out where they are and I'll have money to burn. Yipee.
Merchant 1 (*amused*) My dear Tinbad. *No-one* knows the hiding place of the Forty Thieves. (*He hands the paper back*) If the Calif's own men cannot find it, what chance do *you* have of doing so? Take my advice, old friend. Forget this reward and stick to what you do best—sewing garments.

Everyone agrees

Tinbad (*disgusted*) Huh. It's all right for *you* lot. You've got families. But what about me? I haven't got anybody. Nobody wants to marry a poor tailor.

Merchant 2 Oh, I wouldn't say that, Tinbad. What about Ali Baba's housekeeper, old Cascara? You're exactly the kind of man *she's* looking for. You're breathing.

Everybody laughs

Tinbad Give over. I don't want to marry *her*. She's walked up the aisle so many times, they're trying to make her pay for a new carpet. No ... the one *I* want to marry is the most beautiful girl in Cairo ... (*Dreamily*) Marsaina.

Merchant 2 Marsaina? The slave-girl of that old miser Kassim Baba? (*He laughs*) Why, even if you were the richest man in all Arabia, you'd never get *her* to marry you. Everyone knows she's in love with Haroun, the son of Ali Baba.

Tinbad So what? *He'll* never be able to marry her, will he? He's only a poor woodcutter like his father. And you know as well as I do, unless he can raise enough money to buy her freedom, old Kassim won't even let him visit the house.

Merchant 1 (*nodding sadly*) That's true. Never was a man born with such a love of money as Kassim Baba.

Tinbad So that's why I've got to find out where the Forty Thieves are hiding and claim the reward. Once I'm rich and famous, old Kassim won't be able to sell her to me fast enough.

Merchant 2 Well, we wish you luck, Tinbad. But take care. Al Raschid and his followers are the cruellest, most evil men in Arabia. If they should catch you, expect no mercy.

Tinbad Huh, they don't scare *me*. I come from a family of real fighting men. My eldest brother was so strong, he once went up to (*He names a famous boxer*) and punched him right on the nose. (*He preens himself*)

Merchant 2 (*amazed*) By the beard of the prophet, I must meet this brother of yours. I would like to shake hands with him.

Tinbad (*scornfully*) Don't be daft. I'm not going to dig him up just to shake hands with *you*.

The crowd jeer good naturedly and exit

(*Bewildered*) Here, where's everybody going? Come back. (*Puzzled*) Is it something I said? (*He sees the audience*) Oooh ... tourists. (*Brightly*) Hello.

Audience reaction

Hey ... come on. You can do better than that, can't you? Speak to Tinbad. (*He calls again*) Hello. (*Audience reaction*) Well ... that's a bit better. ... but not much. You're not shy, are you? (*Audience reaction*) Eh? You *are*? Well, we can soon fix that. Listen. We're going to have some *real*

Act I, Scene 1

fun here tonight, and the best way to do it, is for everyone to get to know each other. So what I want you to do is ... everybody turn to the person sitting on your left, and say "Hello. How are you?" (*He encourages them to do this*) Now then. Everybody on the *left* turn to the person on your right and say "Mind your own business, Nosey" (*He laughs*) There. I thought that'd do the trick. Everybody's smiling now. Right, then. Let's have another go. (*He calls*) Hello. (*Audience reaction*) Smashing. We're all mates now. And because we're all mates, I'm going to tell you something. I ...

Cascara, Ali Baba's housekeeper, enters. She is dressed in traditional Dame costume with absolutely no concession to eastern style of dress

Cascara (*spotting him*) Coo-ee. Tinbad. (*She simpers and waves coyly*)
Tinbad (*taken aback*) Oh, hello Cascara. I hardly recognised you in that get-up. What's happening? You're not going to a Fancy Dress Party, are you?

Cascara moves DS *to Tinbad*

Cascara (*beaming*) 'Course not, silly. I got it in the sale at (*She names a local dress shop*). It came all the way from England. It's called "The opportunity dress".
Tinbad Opportunity dress?
Cascara Yes. (*She smooths her bust*) There's plenty of room at the top.
Tinbad Well, if you ask *me*, it's a bit on the tight side.
Cascara Oh, yes. I know. As a matter of fact, it's tighter than my skin.
Tinbad What do you mean, it's tighter than your skin? That's impossible.
Cascara No it isn't. I can sit down in my skin, but I can't sit down in this. (*She simpers*) Anyway, never mind the frock. I was just on my way to your shop to tell you about the terrible experience I had last night.
Tinbad Eh? What terrible experience?
Cascara Well, I'd just gone upstairs to get into me nightie, when I heard this unusual noise. So I looked out of the window, and there he was. A strange feller trying to climb up to my bedroom.
Tinbad Blimey. He *must* have been strange. And what did you do?
Cascara (*primly*) I picked up the telephone and called the Fire Brigade.
Tinbad Eh? What did you want to do *that* for? You should have called the police.
Cascara No, no. It had to be the Fire Brigade. My bedroom's in the attic, you see, and I wanted to know if they could lend him a ladder. (*She sighs*) Oh, it's not easy being a sex-symbol, you know. You never get a minute to yourself. There's always some mad, impetuous feller chasing after you. (*She preens herself*)
Tinbad (*scornfully*) Give over. Who'd chase after you?
Cascara (*stung*) Well, Abdul the farmer would, for one. (*Archly*) Only this morning he told me I reminded him of a cornfield in early Spring. (*She simpers*)
Tinbad Yes. You look like a scarecrow. (*He laughs*)

Cascara glares at him

(*Quickly*) No. I'm only joking. As a matter of fact, every time I look at you, I wonder how you managed to get a figure like that? (*He winks at the audience*)

Cascara (*not noticing*) Well, I suppose it's because I swim a lot. (*She simpers and caresses her thighs*)

Tinbad Oh. So you think swimming helps to give you a good shape, do you?

Cascara I certainly do.

Tinbad Have you ever seen a *duck*?

Cascara (*reacting, then recovering herself*) Oh. It's a good job I know you're only teasing me. (*She beams at him*) But I like a feller with a sense of humour. I couldn't possibly marry you if you didn't have.

Tinbad (*startled*) Marry me?

Cascara (*coyly*) Oh, I've seen the way you look at me when you think I'm not watching. You can't *wait* to propose to me, can you?

Tinbad (*taken back*) Eh? *I* can't wait to propose to *you*?

Cascara (*triumphantly*) You see. I knew it. (*Excitedly*) Ooooooh. He wants to marry me. I can't wait to tell the girls at the club. (*She flutters and preens*)

Tinbad Eh? What club? What club?

Cascara The club I go to every Monday night, of course. (*Frowning*) What's the matter? Don't you believe in clubs for women?

Tinbad Only if kindness fails. (*Worriedly*) I can't marry *you*, Cascara. You're not my type. Besides. I can't *afford* to get married. Business is so bad, even the shoplifters have stopped coming. Unless I can find where the Forty Thieves hide out and claim that reward, I'm going to be bankruptured.

Cascara (*anxiously*) Oh, I say. (*She thinks*) Here, well I'll tell you what. *I'll* come and help you find them, if *you* promise to propose to me as soon as you get the reward.

Tinbad (*not liking the idea*) Oh. But what happens if we *don't* find them? You won't expect me to propose to you *then*, will you? (*He looks at her anxiously*)

Cascara Of course not. I wouldn't dream of it.

Tinbad sighs with relief

I'll propose to you. Come on.

Cascara exits DL *followed by a despondent Tinbad*

As they exit, Ali Baba enters UR. *He is an elderly man, stooped by poverty, dressed in shabby cotton trousers, turban and a much-patched shirt. He carries a bundle of sticks over his shoulders. Moving* DC, *he calls his wares*

Ali Firewood for sale. Firewood for sale. Who'll buy my firewood? (*He looks around and sighs*) Ahyee. Too late again. (*He puts down his wood*) Not a single stick sold. Allah has in truth forsaken Ali Baba. Whatever will I tell my son, Haroun?

Haroun enters UL. *He is a handsome youth in garments as shabby as his father's, but bubbling with life*

Act I, Scene 1

Haroun (*seeing Ali*) Father. (*He hurries down to him*) Did you have any luck?

Ali indicates his wood and shakes his head

(*Kindly*) Never mind. I'm sure you did your best. Another day without food won't do us any harm.

Ali Another day? Then my brother, your Uncle, still refuses to help us?

Haroun I'm afraid so. He even threatened to call the police if we bothered him again.

Ali (*sadly*) So he didn't give you anything—even though he knew we were starving?

Haroun Oh, yes. He threw me a last year's calendar and told me to pick the dates off it. (*Annoyed*) I wouldn't mind so much, but the crumbs from his table would feed half the city for a month.

Ali Now now, Haroun. If it is Allah's will that we are penniless, whilst my brother Kassim lives richly, who are we to complain?

Haroun (*contrite*) Yes, Father. You're absolutely right. But it all seems so unfair, doesn't it? You work so hard and get little in return, whilst he does nothing but count his jewels and possessions. Don't you ever wish *you* were wealthy too?

Ali Oh, yes Haroun. I have my dreams. All my waking hours are filled with them, and even though I know they'll never come true, how pleasantly they pass the time.

Song 2 (Ali)

At the end of the song, Marsaina hurries on UL. *She is a beautiful slave-girl in bright silken clothing and carries a small basket containing fruit and bread*

Marsaina (*calling*) Haroun. (*She hurries down to them*)

Haroun (*surprised*) Marsaina. What are *you* doing here?

Marsaina I came to bring you this. (*She thrusts the basket at him*) Quickly. Take it before someone sees.

Haroun (*taking the basket*) Food. But where did it come from?

Marsaina The kitchen of my Master, Kassim, of course. It's only bruised fruit and stale bread, but I couldn't bear to see it thrown away when I know how desperately you needed something to eat.

Ali May the blessing of Allah fall upon you, Marsaina. But if my brother should find out you've helped us . . .

Marsaina I know. He'll have me punished. But let him. See if *I* care. No man should have food to spare while his own brother starves.

Haroun (*warmly*) We thank you, Marsaina. And one day, I promise, we'll repay you for all you've done for us.

Marsaina (*shyly*) If that is the will of Allah, then so be it. But now I must hurry back before they notice I'm gone.

Marsaina turns to go out

Haroun Wait. When shall we see you again? We'll need to return the basket.

Marsaina (*thinking quickly*) Tonight. Outside the city walls. Wait by the seven palms.

She quickly exits

Haroun (*calling after her*) I'll be there. (*To Ali*) Oh, Father. Isn't she the most beautiful girl in all Arabia?
Ali Without doubt, Haroun. But even though your heart is filled with love for her, 'tis best to forget all thoughts of marriage. Kassim would never allow her to marry a penniless boy like you.
Haroun (*sadly*) I know. But all the same, I can't help feeling that something wonderful is going to happen. (*Puzzled*) There's a strange sort of atmosphere in the market-place today. It's almost as if ... if ... well, someone is watching us. Can't *you* feel it too?
Ali The only thing *I* can feel is my stomach rumbling. Come along, Haroun. Our supply of wood is getting short and we've just time for something to eat before set out to find more.

He picks up his bundle of sticks and begins to exit DL

Haroun (*still puzzled*) It's all around us. (*He looks about*) Something ... magical.
Ali Come along, Haroun.

Ali exits

Haroun Coming, Father.

Haroun takes a last look round and follows

As Haroun exits, the market-place is suddenly flooded with swirling vapour and Morgana, the Mistress of Fates, enters UR. *She is a haughty Immortal, sheathed in voluptuous silks and chiffons, a great cloak cascading from her shoulders. She moves* C

Morgana   From distant realms where neither Time
Nor Tide the course of life dictates,
Come I, the Ruler of them all ...
Morgana, Mistress of the Fates.
Within my hands, the fate of ev'ry
Mortal man doth rest:
And from the day that he is born,
'Tis *I* who puts him to the test.
Each joy and sorrow, rise or fall
By me is thus ordained,
And lest I wish it, fame or fortune
Ne'er by anyone is gained. (*She smiles wickedly*)
But now and then, I change my mind ...
Amusements new to seek ...
Then wealthy lose their riches
And the strong become quite weak.
The wise are extra foolish.

Act I, Scene 1

> The blessed ones are curs'd.
> Whilst beggars in the gutters find
> Their fortunes have been quite reversed.
> And so today, it is my whim
> Some mischief to create.
> The strands of Destiny I'll twist
> And change old Ali Baba's fate. (*She laughs amusedly*)

Avarice, the Afrit, enters L. *In similar attire to Morgana, but dressed in entirely black and green, she is the epitome of evil*

Avarice Hold fast ... before you touch those strands,
I need to have your word
That those *I* rule shall not be harmed.

Morgana How utterly absurd.
As well you know, dear Avarice,
If fortune on one man
Should smile, another suffers.
This has been so since the world began.

Avarice (*wheedling*) Then why not leave things as they are?
No need to interfere.
Let Ali Baba *starve* to death.
No use is he to any here.

Morgana (*amused*) I see. And what of *Al Raschid*?
What use is *he*, I ask?
(*Thoughtfully*) It might be fun to link *their* fates ...
An interesting task. (*She glances sideways at Avarice*)

Avarice (*fuming*) I'm warning you, Morgana ...
I won't stand idly by.
If you persist this foolishness
Then Ali Baba has to die.

Morgana (*coldly*) Harm but one hair of that man's head
And you yourself will come to grief.
Now go. Whilst I the fates entwine
Of Woodcutter and common Thief.

Morgana makes mystic movements in the air as though entwining strands of silk

Avarice So be it, proud Morgana, but
Don't ever say you were not warned.
Your plan, I vow, I'll bring to naught.
Before another day has dawned.

Avarice exits

Morgana (*gleefully*) The threads are joined. The task is done.
Two single lives become as one.
Now watch as paths of Robber Scourge
And Ali Baba meet and merge.

With a delighted laugh, Morgana exits, swirling her great cloak behind her

At the same moment Kassim Baba enters UL. *He is a miserly old man and, though dressed in the best that money can buy, appears to be in great pain as he hobbles* DC *followed by his bossy wife, Rhum Baba*

Kassim (*agonised*) Oooh. Owww. Oooh. Ooooooh. Arghhhh.
Rhum (*irritated*) What on earth's the matter with you, Kassim?
Kassim (*groaning*) It's these shoes, of course. They're five sizes too small and they're giving me corns.
Rhum Then why are you wearing them?
Kassim Because I found a packet of corn plasters this morning and I don't want to waste them. (*He groans*) Owwwww.
Rhum Oh, stop making such a fuss, Kassim. *My* feet are hurting too. I still don't know why we had to run here behind the bus instead of riding inside it.
Kassim Isn't that obvious, my darling Rhum? If we'd ridden *inside* the bus, we'd have had to pay the bus fare. By running *behind* it, we've saved twenty pence each.
Rhum (*annoyed*) Oh, you *fool*, Kassim. Why didn't we run behind a *taxi*? That way we could have saved *ten times* as much.
Kassim (*realising*) Oh, bother. Now I'll be in a bad temper for the rest of the day.
Rhum (*soothingly*) No you won't, dear. No you won't. You'll feel much better when you've done what we came to do.
Kassim (*remembering*) Oh, yes. Yes. Of course. (*He smiles*) I can't wait to give that wretched brother of mine *another* telling off. How dare he send his son to my house to beg for food? Does the man think we're made of money?
Rhum I'm sure he does, dearest heart. And not only that, you must insist he gives Haroun a good whipping, too. With my own eyes, I saw him outside the house doing a terrible impersonation of you.
Kassim (*annoyed*) What? And did you speak to him?
Rhum I certainly did. I told him to stop acting like a fool.

Kassim reacts

Hanki Panki and Jiggeri Pokeri enter UR. *They are dressed in very shabby clothing and look thoroughly down and out*

Hanki (*calling*) Baksheesh. Baksheesh.
Jiggeri (*calling*) Alms for the love of Allah.

They spot Kassim and Rhum and hurry down to them, hands outstretched for money

Rhum (*wrinkling her nose*) Ugh. Beggars. (*To them*) Go away, you horrible smelly creatures.
Hanki (*to Kassim*) Oh, don't send us away, Mister. We're starving. We haven't had anything to eat for days.
Kassim Be off with you. If you want food, you must buy it.

Act I, Scene 1

Jiggeri How can we? We ain't got no money.
Rhum (*snootily*) *Ain't* got no money. You mean you *haven't* any money.
Hanki That's what he said. We ain't got no money.
Rhum No, no. You *haven't* got any money. *We* haven't any money. *They* haven't any money.
Jiggeri Blimey. Ain't nobody got none?
Kassim (*snorting*) Bah. Men like you should be ashamed to be seen begging. Hasn't anyone ever offered you jobs?
Hanki Well, one feller did. But all the rest were a lot more reasonable.
Rhum (*haughtily*) Ooooh. Out of our way, you miserable wretches. You'll get nothing from *us*, I can promise you.

Rhum moves DR *and exits*

Kassim Not a penny. (*He begins to follow Rhum*)
Hanki (*to Kassim*) Wait. Wait. If you won't give us any money for food, how about giving us fifty pence for a nice, comfortable bed?
Kassim (*pausing*) Fifty pence? (*He muses*) Well, I suppose that's not *too* much to ask. (*To Hanki*) Very well. Bring it round to my house, and if it's worth fifty pence, I'll buy it.

He exits DR *haughtily*

Jiggeri (*glaring after him*) Stingy old devil. (*He groans*) Oooh, I'm so hungry I'd even eat a British Rail sandwich.
Hanki Me too. Oh, I wish we were back in Baghdad. I know a restaurant there where you can eat dirt cheap.
Jiggeri Oh, I wouldn't fancy that. Who wants to eat dirt?
Hanki (*hitting him*) Idiot. Now come on. Think. We've got to get money somehow.

Al Raschid enters UR. *He is a sinister individual in dark robes and turban, and a cloak hangs from his shoulders. A fearsome dagger is tucked in his belt. He stands observing Hanki and Jiggeri thoughtfully*

Jiggeri (*not noticing*) Well, perhaps we could open a stall in the market and sell bottles of truth drug.
Hanki Don't be daft. There's no such stuff.
Jiggeri Yes there is. I've just invented it. (*He pulls a small bottle out of his pocket*) Look. One sip of this and you have to tell the truth.
Hanki Let *me* try that. (*He snatches the bottle and drinks, only to spit it out*) Yeukkkk. That's paraffin.
Jiggeri That's the truth. (*He takes the bottle back*)

Raschid moves DS *to them*

Raschid So. Looking for work, eh? Then perhaps *I* can help you?
Jiggeri (*turning to him*) Who are *you*?
Raschid Names are not important, but let's just say that I am leader of the most famous gang of robbers in history.
Hanki (*scornfully*) Gerraway. You don't look a bit like (*He names the leader of a political party*)

Raschid (*annoyed*) Fool. Dolt. Idiot. I am *Al Raschid*, and I lead the Forty Thieves.
Jiggeri Oh. (*To Hanki*) If there's only forty of 'em, he must mean the Social Democrats.
Raschid Bah. Come over here.

They move closer to him

Early this morning, two of my best men were killed by the Calif's soldiers and I need replacements for them quickly. You could be just the ones I'm looking for. Tell me ... Are you tough and ruthless?
Hanki 'Course we are. I'm rough and he's toothless.
Raschid And have you ever demanded money with menaces?
Jiggeri Not half. We used to work for the Inland Revenue.
Raschid Very well. You'll do. Welcome to the fellowship of the Forty Thieves.
Hanki You mean ... you want us to join your gang? Oh ... I don't know about that. We'd have to think about it, wouldn't we, Jiggeri?
Jiggeri Yeah. I mean, how much would you be paying us, for instance?
Raschid Don't worry. I'll pay you what you're worth.
Hanki (*taken aback*) You must be joking. We're not going to work for *that*.
Raschid (*drawing his dagger*) In that case, I'm afraid I'll have to make sure you never speak of this encounter to anyone else.
Jiggeri (*quickly*) Of course ... if you offered us ten pence a week and a bag of doughnuts, we *could* change out minds.
Raschid All right. (*He puts his dagger away again*) I agree. Then follow me ... to the hiding place of the Forty Thieves.

They all exit

Scene 2

The Oasis of the Seven Palms

A lane scene. The backcloth is of a tranquil oasis with a cluster of seven palm trees sheltering it. The city of Cairo is in the background. It is evening and the scene is bathed with the last rays of golden sunlight. (If required this scene can be played in front of secondary "Tabs")

Cascara enters in a new frock

Cascara (*delightedly*) Ooh, I say, girls. Here we are at the oasis of the seven palms. Cairo's answer to (*She names the local lovers' lane*). I haven't been here since me and my last husband were courting. Oh, what a gentleman *he* was. Always kept his eyes shut on crowded buses, you know. Couldn't bear to see a woman standing. And talk about *brave*. I remember him coming home once and telling me he'd seen a great big bully hitting a poor defenceless woman while everybody else just stood around watching. Well, he wasn't having *that*. Not *him*. He walked straight up to the brute and said, "Here, you. Why don't you try hitting a *man* for a change?"

Act I, Scene 2

Well, he never *could* remember what happened after that, but it just shows you the kind of feller he was, doesn't it? (*She looks round*) I wonder where Tinbad's got to? He promised to meet me here to discuss where we're going to search tomorrow, and there might be a chance of a quick kiss and cuddle if I play me cards right.

Tinbad enters R

Tinbad Hello, kids. Sorry I'm late, Cascara, but ... (*He reacts at the sight of her*) Oh, I say. That's an unusual dress you're wearing.
Cascara (*simpering*) Do you like it?
Tinbad Not half. It makes you look just like a chiffonier.
Cascara (*to the audience, pleased*) Oh, I say, girls! Did you hear that? He thinks I look like a chiffon ... (*She realises*) Just a minute. Just a minute. (*To him*) What do you mean, "It makes me look like a chiffonier?" A chiffonier's a big thing with drawers.
Tinbad Well? (*He chortles*)
Cascara (*fuming*) Oooh. And to think I've been stood standing here waiting to waste me feminine wiles on a cut-price tailor, when I could have been passionately pressed to a Persian potentate. (*To him*) All right, then. If that's the way you want it, you can look for the Forty Thieves on your own, tomorrow. *I'll* go to Paris and marry one of them French masseurs, instead.
Tinbad No, no, Cascara. You mean monsieurs. *Monsieurs*. A masseur's one of them fellers who lays you on a table then pats and rubs you all over.
Cascara As I was saying, I'll marry a masseur.
Tinbad Oh, you don't want to go chasing off to foreign countries just because I was pulling your leg. I mean, where would the world be without its little joke?
Cascara (*tartly*) Well *you* wouldn't be alive, for a start.
Tinbad (*soothingly*) Come on, Cascara. Don't be like that. You wouldn't *really* marry somebody else, would you? Not *really*.
Cascara Wouldn't I? Just wait and see.
Tinbad But ... but ... only this morning, you said you wanted to marry *me*.
Cascara You? (*Scornfully*) Hah. The next feller *I* marry's got to be a hero. Afraid of nothing and nobody.
Tinbad Give over, you're not *that* bad.

Cascara reacts

Anyway, *I'll* be a hero after I've found the Forty Thieves, won't I? And everybody round here'll have to start looking up to me.
Cascara Why? Are you going to have your sandals fitted with high heels?
Tinbad No, no. But I could be the new Sherlock Holmes, couldn't I? Helping the police to catch burglars and things.
Cascara (*scornfully*) You?
Tinbad Well somebody's got to do it, haven't they? I mean, I don't know what the country's coming to, these days. There's Income tax fiddling, crooks selling their life stories to newspapers and films, bribery all over the place, and swindlers making fortunes out of people like you and me. I don't know how they get away with it.

Cascara starts to move off

Cascara I do. They get themselves elected.

Cascara exits

Tinbad Eh? (*He begins to follow her off*) Cascara! Wait! Cascara!

Tinbad exits

Marsaina and Haroun enter. Haroun carries the basket used in the previous scene

Marsaina Oh, Haroun, it's been lovely seeing you again, if only for a few minutes. But I'd better be getting back. My Mistress will be calling for me soon to dress her for dinner.

Haroun (*regretfully*) I should be returning home, too. Father hadn't returned from his wood gathering when I left, and I'm starting to get a little bit worried about him. The City gates will shortly be closing for the night.

Marsaina Has he stayed out this late before?

Haroun Well, once or twice. When he had to go to the mountains.

Marsaina (*hopefully*) Then perhaps that's where he went today?

Haroun (*nodding*) It's possible, I suppose. (*He smiles*) But I hope he's had better luck than I have. Only two bundles of sticks sold all day.

Marsaina Poor Haroun. But don't worry. I'll try to bring you more food tomorrow.

Haroun Thank you, Marsaina. Your kindness shall be rewarded in Paradise. (*He gives her the basket*) But be careful. If Uncle Kassim found out you were helping us and we were meeting like this, he'd be furious.

Marsaina (*smiling*) Until tomorrow, then. (*She begins to draw away*)

Haroun Oh, if only I had the money to buy your freedom. You'd never have to set foot in his miserable house again.

Marsaina Perhaps one day, Haroun. But till then I must serve him faithfully or be sold in the slave market.

Haroun (*suddenly*) Perhaps we could run away together? Go to Baghdad.

Marsaina (*shaking her head*) Your uncle is a wealthy man. He would send someone after us. And if we were caught, we'd surely be put to death.

Haroun (*sadly*) You're right, of course. Even if we *did* escape his clutches, he'd make quite sure my father suffered for it. Oh, Marsaina. What are we going to do? Will we never be able to marry?

Song 3 (Haroun and Marsaina)

They exit R

Avarice enters L

Avarice (*sneering*) You fools. No happiness you'll find
Whilst Avarice draws breath.
I'll prove to smug Morgana that
To cross *me* only leads to death.
Old Ali Baba dies tonight ...

Act I, Scene 3

> Of that you may be sure.
> No fortune vast will come *his* way.
> He'll perish as he lived ... quite poor.
> A mighty sandstorm I'll arouse
> Of fury unsurpassed.
> Then lost and hungry, burned and choked
> Shall Ali Baba breathe his last.

She laughs and exits

At that moment, the Lights begin to flicker and a great wind begins to blow. Several citizens and merchants stagger on shielding their faces and calling "Sandstorm! Sandstorm!" This builds to a speedy climax ending with total black-out and great storm effects

Scene 3

Outside the Magic Cave

A rocky gorge in the mountains. Massive boulders are piled high at the foot of a great cliff. Behind one of these is the entrance to the magic cave. Stunted trees stand R and L, masking other entrances. When the scene begins, it is early dawn and Ali Baba is sprawled out on the ground UC, face down. Around him Sand Spirits are posed. Mysterious music plays and the Spirits perform a slow eastern dance with much twisting and twirling

Dance (Sand Spirits)

At the end of the dance, the Spirits strike an attitude and Morgana enters regally. She glances at Ali Baba with a smile, then moves C and faces the audience

Morgana Fear not, for Ali Baba lives ...
> Despite the plans of Avarice.
> By magic *I* protected him
> Until the raging storm did cease.
> His stumbling feet I guided here
> Then cast him into dreamless sleep
> From which, quite soon, he will awake
> His date with Destiny to keep.

With a swirl of her great cape, Morgana exits

The silent Sand Spirits follow her

The Lights brighten and Ali Baba stirs and wakens

Ali (*groaning*) Ooooooh. Where am I? (*He sits up and looks round*) What am I doing *here*? (*He gets to his feet and calls*) Zenobia? Zenobia? Where are you my little donkey? (*He looks round in despair*) Lost. Lost in that terrible sandstorm. Poor Zenobia. And poor Ali Baba. To lose the only possession I had left in the world. Truly Allah has turned his face from me. (*He listens*) But wait. The sound of horses coming this way. Perhaps some passing merchants have found her? I'll attract their attention. (*He hurries* UL *and gazes off*) Ayeee. These are no merchants. Look at the swords they carry. May Allah preserve me ... I'm surrounded by thieves. (*He looks around hastily*) Where can I hide myself?

Ali scuttles DR *and exits behind a tree*

As he does so, the sound of many voices is heard and Al Raschid enters followed by some of the Forty Thieves. All are heavily armed, and some carry bulky sacks over their shoulders. With military precision, they fill the stage, singing lustily

Song 4 (Raschid and Thieves)

At the end of the song, the thieves give a great cheer and relax, leaving Raschid C

Raschid (*laughing harshly*) Ha, ha. Once more we return to our hideaway laden with treasure. (*To Achmed*) Have the guards been posted, Achmed?
Achmed As usual. Twenty on the hilltop. The rest hidden behind the rocks.
Raschid And the two new men?
Achmed (*pointing off* L) Over there. Guarded and blindfolded, as you ordered.
Raschid Good. Until we are sure of them, it would not be wise to reveal our most precious secret ... the hiding place of the Forty Thieves. Have them brought before me at once.
Achmed And if they are not what they appear to be?
Raschid (*giving an evil smile*) Then, my dear Achmed, we slit their throats and lose the bodies in the desert. (*He draws his dagger and strokes the blade*)

Achmed gives a signal and a Robber brings on Hanki and Jiggeri. They are still blindfolded

Jiggeri (*protesting*) Here, not so fast. I can't see where I'm going.
Hanki Slow down a bit, can't you?
Raschid Remove the blindfolds. (*He puts his dagger away*)

The Robber removes the blindfolds, then steps back to join the others. Hanki and Jiggeri blink at the light

(*With a great false smile*) Welcome, my friends. Welcome to the secret hiding place of the Forty Thieves. (*He indicates the area*)
Hanki (*looking around, unimpressed*) Is this it, then? It doesn't look very secret to me.
Jiggeri Me neither.
Raschid (*smiling*) Ah, there's more to this place than meets the eye, my friends—as you'll soon find out. But first, tell us your names.
Jiggeri Well, I'm Jiggeri Pokeri, and he's Hanki Panki.
Raschid I see. And how long have you been following our *honourable profession*?

Act I, Scene 3   15

Jiggeri (*proudly*) Oh we've been robbers for *years*, haven't we, Hanki? In fact, we'd robbed our first bank before we'd left (*He names a local secondary school*).
Raschid (*interested*) Really? And how much did you get?
Hanki Seven slices of bacon.
Raschid (*baffled*) Bacon?
Jiggeri Yes. It was a *Piggy* Bank. (*He chortles*)
Raschid (*glowering*) Have you ever stuck up a stagecoach?
Hanki No. But we've held up an umbrella. (*He cackles*)
Raschid (*smiling*) Ah, my friends, I see you have a sense of humour. That is good. I like a little laugh, myself. In fact, I'll have one *now*.

He begins to laugh. Gradually everyone joins in until Jiggeri and Hanki are laughing hysterically. Raschid suddenly stops, as do the robbers. Raschid turns to Achmed and snarls savagely

Achmed. Strip the flesh from these two idiots and have them staked out in the sun to die.

Jiggeri and Hanki stop laughing

Jiggeri Eh?

He retreats from Achmed

Hanki (*also retreating*) Oooer.

The Robbers draw their daggers and form a circle to surround them

Achmed (*menacingly*) Who wants to be first? (*He waves his dagger*)
Jiggeri (*to Raschid*) Wait, wait. You can't have us killed yet.
Raschid (*snarling*) And why not, may I ask?
Hanki Well, we've got some lines to do in Act Two.
Raschid (*fiercely*) Bah. What do I care about this Act Two? I can do what I like. I am Al Raschid, the most powerful man in Arabia. I have but to breath out the order, and my enemies fall like flies in the dust.
Jiggeri Well there's no need to get embarrassed about it. Everybody has bad breath at times.

Raschid reacts angrily, drawing his own dagger

Hanki (*hastily*) Just a minute. Just a minute. If you kill us now, you'll never find out about the money.
Raschid (*interested*) Money? What money?
Jiggeri (*to Hanki*) Yes, What money? We haven't got a penny.
Hanki (*to Jiggeri*) No, but we know a man who has. Remember that feller we met in the market this morning? The one with the fancy clothes and snooty wife?
Jiggeri (*remembering*) Ooooh, yes. They had more diamonds between them than two packs of playing cards.
Raschid (*very interested*) Diamonds, you say? (*He sheaths his dagger*) Tell me more.

Hanki Well, we don't know who they *were*, but we'd recognise 'em again if we saw 'em. (*To Jiggeri*) Wouldn't we, Jigg?
Jiggeri Not half. Tell your gang to put their pencil sharpeners away, and we'll lead you straight to them.
Raschid (*after a moment's thought*) Agreed. (*He signals to his men*)

The Robbers sheath their daggers

Your lives will be spared if what you say is true. (*To the Robbers*) We return to the City at once. But first, we must hide our latest prizes. (*To Jiggeri and Hanki, with menace*) What you are about to see must be revealed to no man ... for within our hiding place lies the greatest treasure trove ever seen on Earth: gold, silver, diamonds, rubies, emeralds, and pearls from the crown of Neptune himself.

He turns to the hidden entrance and raises his arms

(*Firmly*) Open, Sesame.

There is a great grinding of rock, and the huge boulder moves inwards to reveal the cave behind. The audience should be able to see clearly, vast heaps of treasure trove. Hanki and Jiggeri gape

(*To the Robbers*) Quickly now.

Picking up the sacks etc., the Robbers exit into the cave and vanish from view

Raschid follows them, and is followed in turn by Hanki and Jiggeri

As soon as the stage is empty, Ali Baba's head appears from behind the tree

Ali (*afraid*) Was ever a man so unfortunate as I? First I'm lost in a sandstorm. Then I lose my faithful ass. And now I'm afraid to move in case I'm caught and killed because I accidentally discovered the hiding place of the Forty Thieves. (*Startled*) Oh! They're coming out again.

He vanishes from sight again

The Robbers re-enter from the cave followed by Hanki and Jiggeri, and finally Al Raschid. Raschid turns back to the cave and raises his arms again

Raschid (*loudly*) Close, Sesame.

With a loud grating noise, the boulder closes over the entrance again, and Raschid turns to face front

And now for a fortune in Diamonds. (*He flings out his arm* L) To Cairo.
Robbers (*loudly*) To Cairo.

Song 4, Reprise (Robbers)

The Robbers exit, still singing

As their voices fade away into the distance, Ali Baba emerges from hiding and cautiously moves UL *to watch them move off*

Ali (*relieved*) They've gone. Merciful Allah! I must escape before they come

Act I, Scene 3

back. (*He hurries* UL) But wait! (*He moves back* C) Has the Caliph not offered a reward of ten thousand dinars to the one who leads his soldiers to where the Forty Thieves hide? Then why shouldn't *I* claim it? With such wealth in my pocket, even my brother Kassim would have to kiss the hem of my garments. (*He laughs delightedly then quickly sobers*) And yet, who is to say the Caliph would indeed *pay* the reward. Everyone knows he loves money almost as much as Kassim does. I might end up with nothing for my pains. (*He thinks*) Wait. Wait. I have it. Inside that cave are more riches than I ever dreamed of ... and all stolen. If I were to fill a small sack and hurry home, no-one would be any the poorer for it and Ali Baba would live in luxury for the rest of his life. (*He laughs*) Oh, Haroun, my son. You shall marry your Marsaina after all. (*He turns to face the cave*) Now what were the magic words? (*He thinks*) Ah, yes. (*Loudly*) Open, Sesame.

The cave opens as before, and Ali hurries inside

As soon as he is out of sight, Avarice enters DL *and the lights dim*

Avarice (*glaring after him*) So Ali Baba did not die.
In vain I cast my spell.
But though it seems his luck has changed,
This tale he'll never live to tell.
For with my help, the Forty Thieves
Will soon find out their loss,
And Al Raschid, I guarantee,
Will be *extremely* cross. (*She sneers nastily*)
He'll not stand by whilst unknown thief
His fortune vast decreases ...
He'll track old Ali Baba down
And chop him into little pieces.

She laughs harshly and exits

The Lights brighten. Ali Baba enters from the cave, carrying a small sack

Ali (*panting*) Allah be praised. In this small sack alone is enough wealth to feed half Cairo for a year. If only I had my little ass, Zenobia, I could carry ten times more. (*He shakes his head*) But no. I mustn't be greedy. With what I have here, the house of Ali Baba will become a paradise on earth, and those who live within it, the happiest of mortals. (*He throws the sack onto his shoulder*) And now back to Cairo.

He begins to exit UL, *then stops*

Ah, I almost forgot. (*Loudly*) Close, Sesame.

The cave closes as before

Goodbye, accursed spot, for you'll never see Ali Baba here again.

He exits singing a reprise of his first song

Lights fade to Black-out

Scene 4

A quiet street

Tinbad enters, looking gloomy

Tinbad Hello, kids. Oooh, I am cheesed off. Everything's going wrong for me these days. I've got no customers in me shop and I can't even get a good night's sleep. It's the feller in the room above me, you see. He's a Scotsman, and he clomps up and down all night in his hob-nailed boots playing his bagpipes. I got so mad a few nights ago, I went upstairs and told him if he didn't make less noise I'd call the police. Well, he was ever so apologetic. Promised he'd be a lot quieter in future. Now he plays in his stockinged feet.

The Babes enter happily

Babes (*excitedly*) Tinbad! Tinbad!

They surround him

Tinbad (*brightening*) Oooh, it's the little kiddiwinkies from the Bazaar. Here what are *you* doing out here on your own?
Babe We're looking for you. We want you to tell us a story.
Tinbad (*amused*) A story? But why don't you ask the storyteller in the market for one?
Babe Because we haven't any money to pay him. And in any case, *your* stories are so much better.
Tinbad (*grinning*) Oh, all right, then. Come in a bit closer and I'll tell you the best story I know.

Song 5 (Tinbad and Babes)

At the end of the song, Tinbad ushers the Babes out and exits himself

Haroun and Cascara enter opposite. They move C

Haroun But whatever can have happened to him, Cascara? He's been out all night.
Cascara (*easily*) Oh, I shouldn't worry, love. He'll turn up all right. I had exactly the same trouble with my third husband. Night after night I used to wonder where he was and what he was doing. Then one evening I stayed at home for a change, and there he was.
Haroun Be serious, Cascara. Something terrible could have happened.
Cascara (*gently*) Now, now. There's no point in getting yourself all worked up, is there? Perhaps he went off with some friends last night, and had a drop too much to drink? (*Sagely*) They do, you know. These fellers.
Haroun But how *could* he have? You know we haven't enough money for food, let alone wine.
Cascara It never stopped my eighth husband. (*She rolls her eyes*) Oooh, he did like a drink or two, that one. Used to eat ten pounds of grapes every day because he thought it was wine in pill form. And the trouble he got himself into. Every night, coming home from the pub, he was held up.

Act I, Scene 4   19

Haroun Really?
Cascara (*nodding*) It was the only way he could stay on his feet. I remember one night, he was so tipsy, he staggered into the lift shaft by mistake and fell ten floors into the basement. I leaned through the door and shouted, "What are you doing down there, you fool?", and he shouted back, "Hanging me coat up love, and look out for that first step—it's ever so steep!"

Ali Baba enters, clutching his sack of gold

Haroun (*relieved*) Father.

He hurries to Ali

Ali Haroun. Quickly. Back to the house. I have the most wonderful news for you. (*He drops the sack at his feet*)
Haroun News? But where have you been? We were so worried.
Ali Our worries are over. No more shall I be Ali Baba the woodcutter, but (*Grandly*) Ali Baba, the greatest merchant in all Cairo.
Cascara (*to Audience*) Blimey ... he *has* been drinking.
Ali Cascara. To the market-place. Buy us the biggest and juiciest roasting lamb the butcher has in his shop, wines, vegetables and baskets of the choicest fruits and nuts. Oh, and don't forget the TV Times.
Haroun But Father ...
Cascara Just a minute. Just a minute. Before the fellers in white coats come and take you away: how are we going to pay for it all? American Express?
Ali Ah, yes. Of course. (*He opens the sack*) Take this. (*He reaches into the sack and his hand emerges again clutching several gold pieces*)
Haroun (*awed*) Gold.
Cascara (*reeling*) Oooh, he's robbed the Bank of Scotland. The heads on 'em are still blinking at the light.
Haroun (*to Ali*) How much of it *is* there?
Ali I've no idea. But we can soon find out. Quickly. Hurry to your uncle's house and borrow his kitchen scales. We can weigh it all before anyone else hears of our good fortune and comes a-begging.
Haroun (*doubtfully*) Well, if you say so, Father. But where did it *come* from?
Ali I'll tell you later. But don't worry, Haroun. I didn't steal it from its owner. Now go. Shoo. Shoo.

Haroun exits quickly

(*Handing the gold coins to Cascara*) And you hasten to the market as I told you. (*Delightedly*) Oho, I can't wait to see the expression on Kassim's face when he hears about my good fortune. He'll be green with envy.
Cascara (*surprised*) You're not going to tell *that* nasty piece of work you've come into money, are you?
Ali Tell him? (*He chuckles*) I'm going to *show* him. I'll throw a big party tonight for my friends, and invite Kassim and his wife to join us. *Then* we'll see who's the poor relation. (*He laughs delightedly*) By this time tomorrow, the whole city will know I'm rich.
Cascara (*doubtfully*) Ooh, I hope you know what you're doing.

Ali (*snapping*) Of course I know what I'm doing. And from now on, when I give an order, I want it obeyed at once or there's going to be trouble. Do you understand? Now off you go to the market, and I'll see you at home in half an hour. Is that clear?

Ali picks up the sack and exits

Cascara (*looking after him*) Yes, Ayatollah. (*To audience*) Whatever's got into *him*? (*Worried*) Here, I hope having all this money isn't going to go to his head. He used to be such a nice old man. (*She sighs*) Well, we'll just have to wait and see.

Shaking her head, Cascara exits

Lights fade to Black-out

Scene 5

Outside Ali Baba's house

The exterior of a very shabby hovel in the poor quarter of the city, with other houses of equal shabbiness flanking it. There is a practical door to the building. It is daylight and poorly dressed people rest listlessly, or chat earnestly to the soft strains of eastern music. An eager Rhum Baba enters R, *followed by her husband Kassim.*

Rhum (*urgently*) Hurry, Kassim. Hurry.
Kassim (*tetchily*) I am doing. I am doing.

They are at once surrounded by people

Citizens (*variously*) Alms for the love of Allah. Help us, Kassim. Bread for the starving, *etc.*
Kassim (*waving them away*) Away, you miserable peasants. How dare you speak to us? Have you no shame?
Woman But we haven't eaten for three days.
Rhum That's your own fault. You must *force* yourself. Now out of our way. We have urgent business with my husband's brother.
Kassim Ah, yes. (*He sniffs the air*) I can smell it now. The most beautiful perfume in the world . . . wafting through his doorway on the morning air. (*He almost swoons with pleasure*)
Man Perfume? From the house of Ali Baba? That's a laugh.
Kassim Oh, no, my friends. The perfume *I* smell is not the kind that comes from bunches of flowers or tiny bottles of scent . . . it's the delicious aroma of cold, hard, clinking, clanking . . . *cash.*
Woman (*amazed*) *Money?*
Rhum (*smiling broadly*) Money.

Song 6 (Kassim, Rhum and Chorus)

At the end of the song Ali enters from his house

Act I, Scene 5

Ali What's all the noise about? (*He sees Kassim and Rhum*) Oh. Kassim. Rhum. It's you. (*Uneasily*) What a pleasant surprise.
Rhum (*tartly*) Indeed. (*He glowers*) We want to have words with *you*, Ali Baba.
Ali (*nervously*) Of course. Please step inside. (*He indicates his door*)
Kassim (*indignant*) Inside *that* rat infested hovel? Certainly not. We'll do all the talking we have to do out here.
Ali (*to Citizens*) Please, can you leave us alone for a few moments?

The Citizens exit

Rhum (*to Ali*) And now, Ali Baba, we should like an explanation of this *disgraceful* behaviour. Is it not bad enough my husband should have a woodcutter for a brother? *Now* he has a thief as well.
Kassim (*accusingly*) From who did you steal that gold?
Ali (*flustered*) Steal? I—I—don't know what you mean.
Rhum (*scornfully*) Don't play the innocent with *us*. The moment Haroun came to borrow our kitchen scales we *knew* there was something fishy going on. Since when have *you* had anything to weigh? (*Smugly*) Unknown to him, I smeared the bottom of the pans with grease, and when he returned them, we found grains of gold dust sticking to it. Now tell us where you got this gold, or we're going straight to the Caliph to accuse you of theft.
Ali (*hastily*) Oh, there's no need to do anything like that, dearest Sister-in-law. (*He lowers his voice*) But I can't tell you the story out here in the street. You never know who might be listening. Come inside and have a glass of sherbert and you shall hear exactly how my good fortune came about.
Kassim (*reluctantly*) Oh, very well. If we must, we must. (*Warningly*) But it better be a *good* story.
Ali (*anxiously*) It is. It is. (*He ushers them inside*) The most wonderful story you've ever heard and every word of it true. It all began yesterday morning when I went out collecting firewood and ...

His voice dies away as they exit into the house

Cascara enters DR

Cascara (*pleased with herself*) Oh, I say girls! Doesn't having a bit of money make a difference? You can do all sorts of things you couldn't do before. Do you know, all my life I've wanted to play a musical instrument, so the minute I found out how rich old Ali Baba is now, I asked him if he'd buy a piano. He said, "You can buy anything you want from now on", so I went into a music shop down the street and asked how much they cost. Oooooooh, aren't they expensive? Two thousand pounds. I couldn't believe my ears. I said to the feller behind the counter, "They're a bit pricey, aren't they?" and he said "Well, I suppose so. But you must understand, it takes five hundred elephants a year to make ivory piano keys". (*She shakes her head in amazement*) Do you know, I never realised they could train animals to do things like that.

Tinbad (*entering*) Hello. (*He sees Cascara*) Oh, there you are, Cascara. I've been looking all over for you.
Cascara (*off-handedly*) Yes, well, I haven't been there. I've been down at Tesco's buying all the food for the party.
Tinbad (*surprised*) What party?
Cascara The one Ali Baba's having tonight. He's inviting everybody in the neighbourhood to the biggest knees up in Arabian history. (*She smirks*)
Tinbad And how's he going to pay for it all?
Cascara (*smugly*) Oh, don't you worry yourself. He came into a fortune this morning, and now he's got so much money, he doesn't know what to do with it.
Tinbad Eh? (*Suddenly interested*) Here, does that mean you'll be getting all the wages he owes *you* now? (*He gapes at her*) You're going to be rich.
Cascara (*beaming*) Not half. And the first thing I'm going to do is buy a nice comfortable mattress for me bed. (*She wriggles in anticipation*)
Tinbad A spring one?
Cascara No silly. One I can use all year round. (*She chortles*) Ooh, there's going to be some changes now, I can tell you. (*Coyly*) Abdul the farmer's already asked me out to dinner with him. (*She simpers*) I think he wants to propose to me.
Tinbad (*alarmed*) Eh? But you wouldn't accept him, would you? I mean, you only met him a few days ago.
Cascara I know. but it's not as if he's an absolute *stranger*, is it? One of me girl friends told me *she* was engaged to him for years.
Tinbad Ohhh ... but you wouldn't marry *him* when you know how *I* feel about you?
Cascara (*in mock surprise*) Eh? You? I didn't know *you* fancied me.
Tinbad But I do. I do. You know I'd die for you, Cascara.
Cascara Yes. You keep saying that, but you never *do* it, do you?
Tinbad Oh, come on, Cascara. How about giving me another chance?
Cascara (*with mock reluctance*) Well, all right, then. But on one condition. You've got to tell me what you'd have done, if I'd said I *wouldn't* marry you.
Tinbad I don't know. I don't suppose I'd ever have got married.
Cascara (*flattered*) Don't be silly. There's plenty of other girls in Cairo.
Tinbad I know. But if you wouldn't have me, who would?

Song 7 (Tinbad and Cascara)

At the end of the song, they exit into the house

Haroun and Marsaina enter.

Haroun ... and as soon as I've bought your freedom from Uncle Kassim, we'll be married without delay.
Marsaina Oh, Haroun. You know there's nothing I'd like better, but you must *listen* to me.
Haroun Of course I will. But first I have to tell everyone they're invited to the party tonight.
Marsaina But that's what I want to talk to you about. I think you're making a big mistake.

Act I, Scene 5

Haroun (*mystified*) In what way?
Marsaina If Al Raschid discovers part of his treasure has been stolen, he's sure to try and find out who was responsible.
Haroun (*smiling*) Oh, I don't think *that's* very likely. One small sack out of a huge caveful? He'll never even notice. And besides, even if he did, where would he look? There are thousands of people in Cairo.
Marsaina I know. But how many were poor men one day and rich the next? If your father throws this huge party and tells everyone about his good fortune, then all Raschid has to do is ask and someone is bound to lead him here.
Haroun (*startled*) Oh, my goodness. You're right. We never thought of that. Come on. We've got to warn Father at once.

They hurry into the house

Jiggeri and Hanki enter DL *looking tired*

Jiggeri (*groaning*) Oh, I'm worn out. We must have walked down every street in Cairo looking for that miserable old feller with all the money, and we haven't seen hair nor hide of him.
Hanki I know. (*He looks round*) And I don't think we're going to find him round here, either. It's scruffier than (*He names local run down area*).
Jiggeri So what are we going to do, then? We daren't go back to that Al Raschid and tell him we've had no luck. He'd be so mad, he'd have our heads chopped off.
Hanki How about making a run for it? We could slip out of the city by a side gate, and go back to Baghdad.
Jiggeri How can we, you fathead? We've got no money.
Hanki We could earn it in *Baghdad*. I heard about one feller there who was determined to be rich so he worked twenty-five hours a day, eight days a week, fourteen months a year ... and even though he started with nothing, by the time he was sixty five, he owned the biggest daily newspaper in Arabia.
Jiggeri Well that's not much, is it? A newspaper only costs twenty-two p.

Al Raschid enters UL

Raschid (*with menace*) Well? Have you found him?
Hanki (*nervously*) Er, not yet, boss. But we're on his trail. Aren't we Jigg?
Jiggeri Oh, yes. Give us another few minutes, and we'll lead you straight to him.
Raschid Good. Because if you *don't* ... (*He draws his dagger*)

Kassim and Rhum enter from the house in deep conversation

Hanki (*surprised*) Boss. Boss. It's him.
Raschid (*seeing them*) Quickly. Hide, and we'll follow him.

Raschid, Jiggeri and Hanki exit DL

Rhum (*delightedly*) Just think, Kassim, all that money, and unable to spend it in case the Forty Thieves find out. (*Smugly*) That'll teach them to give themselves airs. (*Her eyes narrow*) All the same, I don't like the idea of them *having* more money than us.

Kassim Don't worry, dear Rhum. It won't be for long. My stupid brother told me everything. Now I know exactly where this magic cave is, *and* how to get into it. I'll take six of my strongest horses and go there immediately. By the time I return home tonight, even the Caliph himself will not be as rich as I. Then once the treasure is safely stored, I'll tell the soldiers where to find the Forty Thieves, and claim the reward for that, also. (*He cackles delightedly*) Come. We must saddle up the horses at once.

They hurry off in good humour

Raschid and the others emerge

Raschid (*suspiciously*) Strange. Why would such wealthy looking people be here in a place like this? Bah. If only we'd been close enough to hear what they were saying. But no matter. (*To Jiggeri and Hanki*) Follow them at once whilst I find the rest of the Thieves. And lose them at the cost of your lives.

Raschid exits UL

Jiggeri and Hanki follow Kassim and Rhum

Haroun, Marsaina, Ali, Cascara and Tinbad enter from the house looking downcast

Ali (*sighing*) Ayee. Was ever a man so unfortunate as I? A sackful of gold and jewels in my house and I'm still as poor as ever I was.
Marsaina (*kindly*) Not if you're very careful. Spend only one piece of gold at a time in different places of the city, and that way you'll raise no-one's suspicions.
Haroun But what about *us*, Marsaina? Without the money, I'll never be able to buy your freedom. We'll be separated for the rest of our lives.
Cascara Oh, cheer up, everybody. We're no worse off than we were yesterday, and at least we've got something to eat.
Tinbad Cascara's right. And if you tell the Caliph's soldiers where the Forty Thieves hang out, you're bound to get *something* as a reward, aren't you?
Haroun (*realising*) Of course. Then once we've *got* some money, no-one will be surprised if we start spending it.
Marsaina And with Al Raschid in jail, you'll be perfectly safe.
Ali (*cheering up*) Then our troubles are over. I'll go see the Caliph first thing tomorrow morning.
Cascara And in the meantime, we'll have a private little party of our own.

Song 8 (Cascara, Tinbad, Ali, Haroun, Marsaina)

As the first few lines of the song are sung, the Chorus enter gradually, smiling and amused at the levity taking place. As the song progresses, they join in, with dancers also taking their places. The song then builds into a rousing Finale to Act I

CURTAIN

ACT II

Scene 1

The market-place

As before. Daylight. Once more the market place is crowded, the delighted populace watching an energetic sand-dance performed by dancers in the style of Wilson, Keppel and Betty, the Music Hall stars. If this is not possible, a song may be substituted

Dance (Speciality dancers)

At the end of the routine (or song) Ali Baba and Haroun enter UR *Ali is still dressed in his "poor" clothes, and appears somewhat worried. They move* DC *through the animated, but muted, crowd*

Ali (*brushing at his clothes*) Are you sure I look all right, Haroun? Is my face clean and my turban wound properly?
Haroun (*patiently*) Yes, yes, yes, Father. Now *do* stop worrying.
Ali (*still worried*) It's all right for you, but I've never been to the Caliph's palace before and I want to make a good impression. (*Suddenly*) Suppose he won't see me?
Haroun Of course he will. As soon as he knows you've brought him the information he wants, he'll greet you with open arms. Now off you go.
Ali (*nodding*) Very well. Oh, and you'd better take your uncle Kassim the money I promised him in return for his silence.
Haroun I'm surprised he didn't want it all, the miserable old miser. (*He glances off* L) But there's no need for *me* to take it. Here comes Aunt Rhum. She's probably on her way to collect it now.

Rhum enters DL *in a fluster*

Rhum Oh, dearest Brother-in-law, Ali. You've got to help me.
Ali Help you? In what way?
Rhum (*glancing around*) Shhh. I'll get rid of the crowd. (*To Crowd*) Quickly. A great merchant waits at the City gates to buy everything you have to sell.

There is an excited flurry in the market-place and all hurry off eagerly

My husband Kassim ... your brother. He's vanished. (*She bursts into tears*)
Ali (*puzzled*) But how? When?
Rhum Yesterday afternoon. After we left your miserable hovel. He saddled six of his finest horses and set out for the magic cave to help himself to whatever treasure was left. (*She cries even harder*)

Haroun (*indignantly*) Why, the crafty old twister.

Ali (*to Rhum*) And you haven't seen him since, dear sister-in-law?

Rhum (*sniffling and shaking her head*) Not a glimpse. And I've waited all night. Oh, my poor Kassim. Whatever has become of him? (*She sobs again*)

Ali (*to Haroun*) I must go to the cave at once, Haroun. He may have been captured by the Forty Thieves and lie bound and gagged somewhere inside it.

Haroun Well it serves him right if he has. It's his own fault for being so greedy. Besides, why *should* you try to help him? He's never done anything for you but make your life a misery.

Ali (*sighing*) I know. But he *is* my brother. And if it hadn't been for me, he'd never have gone looking for the cave in the first place. I *have* to help him. (*To Rhum*) May I borrow one of Kassim's horses?

Rhum (*tearfully*) Borrow anything you like. Just bring Kassim back to me.

Ali I'll do my best. (*To Haroun*) Look after her till I return. (*He hurries off* L)

Haroun (*reluctantly*) Come along, Aunt Rhum. I'll take you back home.

He escorts the weeping Rhum off L

As they exit, Tinbad enters DR

Tinbad Hello. (*He glances around*) Here, where's everybody gone? I wanted to buy a bag of Turkish Delight to cheer meself up. Well, I'm a bit depressed this morning, you see. I was counting up the money in my till and I accidently swallowed a pound coin, so I thought I'd better go to the doctor's to see if he could get it back for me. Well, he looked right down me throat but he couldn't see anything, so he told me I'd better go to the Income Tax office instead. I said "The Income Tax office? What do I want to go there for?" He said "Well, that lot'll get money out of anybody"!

Cascara enters UR *looking slightly unwell*

Oh, hello, Cascara. (*He notices*) Here, are you all right? You look terrible.

Cascara (*moving down to him*) I know. I've just been on one of those railway trains and it really upset me.

Tinbad Why's that? There wasn't an accident, was there?

Cascara No, no. Nothing like that. It was just that I had to sit with my back to the engine, and whenever I do that, I go all queasy inside.

Tinbad Well, why didn't you change seats with the person opposite?

Cascara I couldn't. There was nobody sitting there. Oh, and I was dying for a drink. But you know how it is when you're not feeling well? I daren't stand up to go for one, so I asked this sweet little Arab boy if *he'd* bring me something.

Tinbad And did he?

Cascara Oh yes. He came back with a lovely big glass full of water and I swallowed it in one gulp. The only trouble was . . . it was so nice I wanted some more, so I asked him to go and get me another one. Well, off he went, and this time, he came back with an *empty* glass. So I asked him what was wrong.

Act II, Scene 1

Tinbad And what did he say?
Cascara He said he couldn't get me one for a minute because there was a feller sitting on the well.
Tinbad (*after a startled reaction*) Anyway, what were you doing on a train?
Cascara Oh, I'd been to Baghdad. To visit my sister. She wrote to me last week, you see, and told me she'd just had a baby. So I *had* to go, didn't I?
Tinbad What? All that way just to see a baby?
Cascara Well, what else could I do? I mean, she forgot to tell me whether it was a boy or a girl, so I didn't know if I was an auntie or an uncle.
Tinbad Here, and talking about uncles. There's a story going round the bazaar, that Kassim Baba hasn't been home all night and nobody knows where he is.
Cascara Oh, I shouldn't take any notice of that. You know what they're like in the bazaar. Always spreading rumours about *somebody*. Last week they were saying Caspar the Coffee-seller had gone mad and thought he was a parking meter.
Tinbad And wasn't it true, then?
Cascara 'Course it wasn't. And he'd have told them so himself if he hadn't had his mouth full of coins. Anyway, never mind about that. You've not forgotten you're taking me out tonight, have you?
Tinbad (*surprised*) Eh? Taking you out? What for?
Cascara To celebrate our engagement, of course. Oooh, I am looking forward to it. A romantic, candle-lit dinner for two . . . a few sips of wine . . . and then . . . (*She puckers her lips and lowers her lashes*) l'amour.
Tinbad (*startled*) L'amour?
Cascara (*passionately*) Tonight, for sure.

Song 9 (Cascara and a reluctant Tinbad)

At the end of the song, Cascara pursues Tinbad as he makes a rapid exit

Morgana sweeps into the market-place with a flourish of her great cape

Morgana A plague on that vile Avarice. How dare she interfere
With things that don't concern her? Well, that slip will cost her dear.
'Twas through *her* intervention sly, that Kassim and his wife
Discovered Ali's secret and in peril placed that poor man's life.
However, thanks to me, that dreadful danger now is past.
I snapped a thread of Destiny, and Kassim Baba breathed his last.

Avarice enters L

Avarice What's that, you say? Kassim is dead?
Morgana Quite so. The game is won.
In peace shall Ali Baba live
As will Haroun, his son.
Avarice Oh, no, my dear Morgana,
You claim vict'ry far too soon.

The Forty Thieves will claim their lives
Before the next full moon.
For this I vow, although he's dead,
Kassim will lead the way
To Ali Baba's dwelling place!
And now, my friend, good day.

Avarice exits

Morgana Whatever can the creature mean?
She makes no sense at all.
And yet, I'd best be on my guard
Lest unexpected things befall. (*She raises both arms in supplication*)
Come, Sands of Time. Fly quickly by.
Let night's dark cloak descend.
The tale of Ali and his son
To bring to happy, peaceful end.

Lights fade rapidly to sunset

Morgana exits with a sweep of her cloak

Haroun and Marsaina enter DR

Haroun It's been *hours* since he left, Marsaina. Perhaps I should borrow a horse and go to look for him?

Marsaina (*worried*) I don't know. The light's almost gone and by the time you reach the mountains, it will be too dark to see anything without a torch.

Haroun Then I'll take one with me.

Marsaina But if the Forty Thieves should see its flame, you'd be in terrible danger. Everyone knows how evil they are. You wouldn't stand a chance against *all* of them.

Haroun I know. But I've got to find out what's happened to my father and Uncle Kassim.

Marsaina (*pleading*) Just wait a while longer. Until the moon rises. Then if they still haven't returned ...

Haroun (*agreeing*) All right. I don't suppose a *few* more minutes will matter. (*Warmly*) Oh, Marsaina, in spite of everything that's happened today, they've been the happiest hours of my life. For the very first time we've been able to spend more than a few fleeting moments together, and even if it never happens again, I'll remember them till the day I die.

Marsaina And so will I, Haroun. But I fear that once Kassim returns, it will be even *more* difficult for us to meet. With all his newfound wealth, he'll never allow you to buy my freedom.

Haroun Don't worry. I'll find a way to do it somehow. Even if he surrounds you with a thousand guards, he'll never keep us apart for long.

Marsaina (*sadly*) If only that were possible.

Haroun It *is*. I swear it.

Act II, Scene 1

Song 10 (Haroun and Marsaina)

At the end of the song, Ali hurries in. He is looking most unhappy and worried

Ali (*gasping*) Haroun . . . Marsaina. (*He totters towards them*)
Haroun (*relieved*) Father. Thank goodness you're back. But where's Uncle Kassim?
Ali (*wailing*) Ayeee. Dead. Chopped into pieces by those murderous bandits and nailed to the walls of the magic cave.
Haroun ⎱ (*together*) ⎰ (*shocked*) What?
Marsaina ⎰   ⎱ Oh, no (*She bites her knuckles*)
Ali (*groaning*) It was horrible. Horrible. I reached their hideout just in time to see the Forty Thieves and their leader riding off into the desert. There was no sign of Kassim so, speaking the magic word, I opened the door and went inside. Poor Kassim. There he was before my very eyes. They must have left him there as a warning to others who discovered their secret.
Marsaina What monsters they must be.
Ali (*nodding*) Monsters indeed, Marsaina. How I wept for him. Then realising my own danger if they returned and found me, I emptied one of the treasure sacks onto the floor, placed the pieces of his body inside it and made my way back across the desert.
Marsaina (*concerned*) How shall we tell Aunt Rhum?
Ali (*sighing*) I'll go there now. We must have a funeral, of course, and the sooner the better.
Marsaina Wait, you may *still* be in danger. When the Forty Thieves arrive back at the cave, they'll know at once that someone has been there. (*Realising*) They could be searching for you, even now.
Haroun Don't worry, Marsaina. They'll never discover who removed to body. It's absolutely impossible.
Marsaina Not at all. If they hear Kassim Baba, the wealthiest merchant in Cairo, has been buried in pieces, it will quickly lead them to the house of his brother.
Ali (*realising*) She's right. They'll chop *me* to pieces, too. (*He wails*)
Haroun (*worried*) What are we going to do?
Marsaina I have an idea. Quickly. Come with me.

Marsaina hurries off R, *followed by Haroun and a stricken Ali Baba*

Al Raschid and some of the Forty Thieves enter UL, *daggers drawn. Jiggeri and Hanki enter with them*

Raschid (*snarling*) So, yet another has discovered our secret hiding place. But I swear by the beard of the Prophet, he shall not live to visit us again. His tracks led us to this miserable city where he hopes to escape our vengeance, but no matter where he hides, we'll seek him out and make him pay. (*To the others*) Go, search the streets and don't return without him.

The Robbers exit variously

Before the sun rises in the morning, that miserable son of a camel will feel the full wrath of Al Raschid and his faithful Forty Thieves.

Raschid exits with a harsh laugh

Lights fade quickly to Black-out

Scene 2

The Street of Lesser Merchants

A lane scene. Cloth depicts tumbledown shops in eastern style. If this is not possible, the scene can be played in front of secondary "Tabs". It is night. Ali Baba and Haroun enter R furtively. They move C, looking cautiously around, then, seeing nothing, Haroun signals silently R. Marsaina appears R, leading Tinbad by the hand. Tinbad is wearing a long nightshirt and clutches a teddy bear. A blindfold is covering his eyes

Tinbad Hang on a minute, missis. Hang on. How much further do we have to go?

Marsaina Only a short distance, I promise you.

Tinbad Well, I hope so. I'm getting cold like this. You might at least have given me time to get dressed. I don't know where the draught's coming from, but I *do* know where it's going. (*He shivers*) Brrrrr.

Marsaina I'm sorry. But as I told you, the task you have to do is very urgent. Every second counts.

Tinbad Yes. But if you'd take this blindfold off me, I could see where I was going and we'd get there a lot quicker.

Marsaina I'm afraid that's out of the question. Not even *you* must know where I'm taking you. But once the job's done, you can return home without delay, so *hurry*. (*She attempts to pull him along*)

Tinbad (*holding back*) Well whose body is it? The one you want me to sew together?

Marsaina What does it matter? All you have to do is sew each piece together as I hand them to you, then take your money and return home again.

Tinbad But I've got to wear this blindfold all the time?

Marsaina Exactly. (*Scornfully*) Unless the task is too *difficult* for you.

Tinbad (*indignant*) Too difficult? I'm the best tailor in Cairo, I am. And if *I* can't sew a body together without looking at the pieces, then *nobody* can. I've had half the folk round here in stitches. (*Curious*) Hey, and talking about folk round here. Don't I *know* you? I'm sure I've heard your voice before. Is it all right for me to have a peep?

Marsaina (*sharply*) No. Certainly not. But touch that blindfold and I'll (*She hesitates a split second*) plunge this *dagger* into your heart.

Tinbad reacts in fright

Now come. (*She pulls his hand*)

Act II, Scene 2

Tinbad Oh, all right then. No need to pull me arm off. (*He follows her*) You *did* say twenty gold pieces, didn't you? I mean, I didn't make a mistake about *that*?

Ali and Haroun exit L *followed by Marsaina and Tinbad, who is still asking questions*

A moment later, Jiggeri and Hanki enter R, *looking rather unhappy*

Jiggeri Oh, I'm fed up with this. Wandering round back streets in the middle of the night instead of being tucked up in a nice warm fireplace.
Hanki Same here. If it wasn't for ... Tucked up in nice warm *fireplace*? What are you talking about? You don't go to bed in a fireplace.
Jiggeri Yes, I do. I've always slept like a log.
Hanki (*pushing him*) Shut up, and come here. (*He pulls him closer*) Now listen. I don't know about you, but I think we've made a big mistake joining this gang. I didn't know we were going to go round *killing* people. I thought we'd be doing *reasonable* things, such as robbing the general public.
Jiggeri (*agreeing*) Yes. Sort of ... doing like the Government does.
Hanki So what do you think we should do?
Jiggeri I think one of us should go back and tell that Al Raschid feller we've resigned from his rotten old gang.
Hanki And so do I. I'll wait here while you do it.
Jiggeri Right. (*He begins to exit then realises*) *Me*?
Hanki Why not? It was your idea. (*Scornfully*) You're not *scared* of him, are you?
Jiggeri (*blustering*) Me? Scared? You must be joking. When I was in the Foreign Legion, the Captain lined us up and asked for somebody to step forward and volunteer for a top secret, highly dangerous mission, (*Smugly*) and *I* was the one who got the job.
Hanki (*in disbelief*) You? Come off it. *You* stepped forward for something dangerous.
Jiggeri No. Everybody else stepped back.
Hanki (*tiredly*) Ooh, why don't you grow up, stupid?
Jiggeri I have done. But I'm not *that* stupid. You don't think that Al Raschid's going to let us pack this job in and walk away, do you? By the time he's finished with us, we won't be able to *crawl*.
Hanki (*worried*) You're right. So what are we going to do? We either stay here and do everything he tells us to, or we make a run for it and try to lead honest lives somewhere else. Right?
Jiggeri Right.
Hanki So let's spend a couple of minutes reviewing the situation.

Song 11 (Hanki and Jiggeri)

Hanki and Jiggeri exit R *at the end of the song*

Lights fade quickly to Black-out

Scene 3

The market-place

As before, but this time it is early morning and the sun is just rising. The market-place is deserted

Avarice enters UL, *looking baleful and moves* DS

Avarice Confound those stupid Forty Thieves.
I vow they must be blind.
All night they've searched for him they seek
Yet *still* they do not find.
A lending hand I'll have to give
To end their tiresome quest.
Despite Marsaina, this day *shall*
See Ali Baba laid to rest.

Avarice exits DL *in a temper*

Cascara and Rhum enter UR

Cascara Now you're quite sure you know what to do, aren't you? You've got to tell everybody that Kassim's ill in bed with blood poisoning, (*She pauses*) and if anybody asks how he got it, tell them he bit his tongue.

Rhum (*protesting*) But what about tomorrow?

Cascara Tomorrow, you can tell them all he died during the night. That way nobody will ever know he was murdered by the Forty Thieves and we'll all be safe.

Rhum (*annoyed*) Oh, thank goodness no-one will ever get to hear of this. Think of the disgrace if anyone found out. How dare he get chopped into little pieces by common criminals?

Cascara (*shrugging*) Well, that's him, all over. (*Realising*) I mean, not *now*, he isn't. He's all sewn together again and good as new. But remember, you haven't to breath a word about this to anybody. Mum's the word.

Rhum (*indignantly*) You don't think I'm going to go round *boasting* about this, do you? Stupid old woman.

Cascara (*startled*) I beg your pudding? (*sweetly*) You ... er ... you wouldn't like to do me a little *favour*, would you, *dear*?

Rhum What kind of favour?

Cascara Stand in front of a steam-roller so I can use you for a book-mark.

Rhum (*indignantly*) Oh. (*Contrite*) Oh, I'm sorry, Cascara. I don't know what's the matter with me. I couldn't have managed without your help. Let's be friends, shall we?

Cascara (*doubtfully*) Well ...

Rhum Oh, *do* say yes. After all, we've known each other ever since we were the same age.

Cascara (*reluctantly*) Oh, all right, then. But no more name calling. From now on we're going to be bosom buddies.

Song 12 (Cascara and Rhum)

As the song ends, they exit DL *arm in arm*

Act II, Scene 3

A moment later Tinbad appears UR. *He is still in his nightshirt and carrying the teddy bear plus a small bag of gold*

Tinbad Hello. Hey, you'll never guess what. I'm *rich*. Some woman paid me twenty pieces of gold for doing an emergency sewing job. (*He shows the bag*) Mind you, it wasn't easy. I had to do it with a blindfold over me eyes and it took all night before I'd finished. Still... twenty pieces of gold. (*He chortles*) I wonder what I should do with it? When I was a little boy, me dad used to make me *save* all my pocket money. I had to put it in this tin box under the stairs. I was seventeen before I found out it was the gas meter.

Al Raschid and Achmed enter behind Tinbad

(*Gloating*) Twenty pieces of gold. Just for sewing a dead body together. (*He chuckles*) I can't believe it.

Raschid and Achmed react

Just wait till I show all the other merchants *this*.
Raschid (*clearing his throat pointedly*) A-hem.

Raschid moves down to Tinbad

Tinbad (*turning to see him*) Oooh, it's (*He names an unpopular public figure*).
Raschid (*hiding his anger*) Ha, ha, ha. I...er...I couldn't help overhearing what you were saying just then. Something about sewing a dead body together, was it?
Tinbad That's right. (*Remembering*) Oh, but I'm not supposed to tell anybody about it. It's a secret, you see. Nobody's got to know.
Raschid (*agreeing*) Of course not. I won't breath a word. (*He smiles savagely*) Whose body *was* it, might I ask?
Tinbad Oh, I don't know *that*. They made me wear a blindfold all the time so I wouldn't recognise him.
Raschid (*aside*) Curses. (*To Tinbad*) But why did you have to sew him together again?
Tinbad Well, I think he'd had a nervous breakdown and gone to pieces. Here, I don't suppose *you've* anything you need sewing, have you? I'm the best tailor in Cairo, you know.
Raschid (*craftily*) Well, I *may* have. But before I ordered anything from you, I'd like a recommendation from a satisfied customer. Perhaps the person who paid you the twenty pieces of gold would oblige?
Tinbad Ooh, yes. (*He thinks*) The only thing is though... I don't know where she lives. I had the blindfold on all the time.
Raschid But surely an *intelligent* person like you could find his way there again—providing you were wearing another blindfold? And for a *hundred* gold pieces...
Tinbad (*awed*) A hundred? (*Hastily*) Where's your handkerchief?

Raschid moves quickly to Achmed and whispers

Raschid Let this idiot guide you to where the body lies hidden, and make a chalk mark on the door so we'll be able to recognize it again. I'll gather the rest of the men and meet you here shortly.

Raschid produces a large handkerchief. He blindfolds Tinbad and pushes him towards Achmed

Go with my friend, tailor. Show him the house and the hundred gold pieces are yours.

Achmed leads Tinbad off UR

(*Drawing his dagger*) And now to prepare ourselves for a meeting with this plunderer of our magic cave. Soon all Arabia shall know how swift the vengeance is of Al Raschid and the Forty Thieves.

He laughs harshly and exits DL

Morgana enters UR

Morgana Because of Avarice, it seems, my plan will go awry.
But fear you not, she won't succeed, and here's the reason why.
The thread of Fate containing Al Raschid and Ali's life
Shall now embrace another, who will end this tale of strife.

She raises her arms

Marsaina, humble slave, to *you* the task I now bequeath
Of ridding us of Forty Thieves ... and Al Raschid, their Chief.

Morgana exits with a light laugh

Ali and Haroun enter DR

Ali Oh, Haroun, my son. All our problems are over now. As soon as Kassim is buried, I'll be the most respected man in Cairo. Ali Baba! A prince among commoners! (*He beams with delight*)

Haroun (*puzzled*) I don't understand.

Ali It's as plain as the nose on your face. As Kassim's brother, all his wealth and possessions come to me, for as you know, in Arabia, that is the law. And with the treasure I took from the cave of the Forty Thieves, I'll have more money than the Caliph himself. (*He chortles*)

Haroun But what about Aunt Rhum?

Ali (*generously*) Oh, I shall have to look after *her*, of course, but Kassim's house is big enough for all of us to live in comfort.

Haroun I think Marsaina and I would prefer a house of our own. After all, once we're married ...

Ali (*interrupting*) Married? (*He laughs*) What nonsense is *this*? The son of a wealthy merchant marrying a common *house-slave*. Why, it's out of the question. We'd be the laughing stock of Cairo.

Haroun (*surprised*) What?

Ali (*smiling*) No, no, no, no, no. We'll find you a bride more in keeping with your new position in life. Perhaps even a princess, eh?

Act II, Scene 3

Haroun (*protesting*) But I don't want a princess, Father. I love Marsaina.
Ali (*annoyed*) You dare to argue with me, Haroun? Let me remind you that *I* give the orders from now on. You will do as I say. Forget this slave-girl and prepare yourself to marry the one I choose for you. Is that understood?
Haroun (*defeated*) Yes, Father.
Ali Good. And now I'm off to look over my new house. Tomorrow night we shall have a magnificent feast to celebrate my good fortune, and the whole city will be invited to join us.

Ali swaggeringly exits DL

Haroun (*miserably*) What am I going to do? How can I tell Marsaina I'm to marry someone else? Oh, if only Father had never found that magic cave. When we were poor, at least I could dream, but now there's nothing to look forward to but a lifetime of memories.

Song 13 (Haroun)

At the end of the song Haroun exits sadly L

Jiggeri and Hanki cautiously enter DR

Hanki (*glancing round*) Quick. Through the market-place and out of the city gates.
Jiggeri (*hesitating*) Do you think we should leave him a note to say we've resigned?
Hanki Of course not, you fathead. We haven't got time.
Jiggeri We could write it in shorthand.
Hanki Idiot. This is the seventh century. Shorthand hasn't been invented yet.
Jiggeri Yes it has. My brother's been writing shorthand for years.
Hanki How could he?
Jiggeri He had his fingers chopped off.

Hanki glances UL

Hanki Look out. Somebody's coming.

As they panic, Achmed enters UL

Achmed (*spotting them*) Aha. (*He moves towards them*) You. Where's Al Raschid? I must tell him his plan succeeded. The tailor led me straight to the house of the man who stole the body from our cave, and I've made a large cross on the door so we can easily find it again.
Jiggeri (*nervously*) We haven't seen him since last night, have we, Hanki?
Hanki (*hastily*) No. No. Not a sign of him.
Achmed I'd better go look for him. You stay here and keep watch.

Achmed exits DL

Jiggeri Quick. Let's hop it before he comes back.

Hanki looks UR

Hanki Too late. There's somebody else coming.

Marsaina enters UR

Marsaina (*seeing them*) Excuse me, but you haven't seen any children playing around here, have you?
Hanki Children? (*He thinks*) No. Why?
Marsaina One of them has chalked a huge cross on the door of that house over there, (*She indicates off* UR) and I want to know why.
Jiggeri Oh, that wasn't children, miss. It was Achmed the 'Orrible. It's to show him which house the tailor led him to, you see.
Marsaina The tailor? Oh, no. (*Aside*) Allah preserve us. We're all in terrible danger.

Marsaina turns and hurries off again UR

Hanki (*puzzled*) What's wrong with *her*?
Jiggeri Don't ask me. But she didn't half look worried.
Hanki She's not half as worried as me. If the rest of the gang come back and find us still here, we'll never be able to escape. Come on! Let's get to the gate.

As they turn to exit, Raschid, Achmed, and three of the Thieves enter. All have their daggers drawn. Hanki and Jiggeri freeze

Raschid There's no time to wait for the others. We must kill the dog who ventured into our cave, and leave before it's too late. Even now the market is beginning to stir. (*To Achmed*) Lead us to the door you marked.
Achmed Follow me.

Achmed hurries off UR *followed by Raschid and the others*

Hanki and Jiggeri still stand-afraid to move

(*Off*) Here's the cross I marked.
1st Thief (*off*) No. It's on this door here.
Raschid (*off*) Fool. It's over here on this door.
2nd Thief (*off*) There's one here, too.
3rd Thief (*off*) And here.
Achmed (*off*) There's crosses on *every* door.
Raschid (*off*) Fool. Dolt. Idiot. We've been tricked.

Raschid re-enters UR, *followed by Achmed and the others. All look furious*

Someone must have seen you marking the door and marked all the others in the same way. Now we'll have to pay that accursed tailor to lead us there again—and this time there'll be no mistake. Find him at once.
Achmed (*glancing off*) Too late. The market-traders are coming.
Raschid (*snarling*) Ten thousand curses. Quickly! We must hide. Find the others and return to the cave. I'll meet you there later.
Achmed What are you going to do?
Raschid I'll disguise myself as a merchant and mingle with the crowd. Perhaps I'll hear something to our advantage. Now hurry.

Act II, Scene 4

Achmed and the others exit, followed by the reluctant Hanki and Jiggeri

Raschid exits DL *as the traders begin to enter, chattering and displaying their wares*

As the area fills Tinbad strolls in, dressed in eye-popping new clothes. Everyone gapes at him

Tinbad Hello.
Merchant (*astounded*) By the great hind leg of a Coptic Camel. It's Tinbad! Tinbad the tailor.

The market-place buzzes with excitement

Tinbad (*holding up a hand*) No, no. You've got it all wrong. From now on I'm finished with tailoring. Starting today I'm going to live in the lap of luxury and do nothing but eat, drink and be merry. (*Delightedly*) Oho. I can't wait to see everyone's faces when they get a load of *this* lot. (*He indicates his clothes*)

Song 14 (Tinbad and Chorus)

Black-out

Scene 4

A quiet street

As before. Daylight

Haroun and Marsaina enter L *and move to* C

Haroun Hurry, Marsaina. We have to tell Father at once. (*He attempts to lead her off* R)
Marsaina But there's nothing to worry about, Haroun. With crosses on *every* door, they'll never be able to find him. He's perfectly safe.
Haroun Provided Tinbad doesn't lead them to him again. (*Grimly*) Just wait till I get my hands on that idiotic tailor.
Marsaina Oh, you mustn't blame Tinbad. He'd never have done it if he'd known whose body it was he'd sewn together. And besides, even if he *did* lead them there again, it wouldn't do any harm. By this time tomorrow you'll be living in Kassim's house and all the Thieves will find is an empty building.
Haroun (*relieved*) Of course. (*Determinedly*) But even so, we must tell Father what you did. You've saved his life *again*, Marsaina, so I don't see how he can possibly object to our getting married now.
Marsaina I wish that were so, Haroun, but what he said was true. I *am* only a slave-girl, and for the son of a rich man to marry someone like me would cause great merriment in the city. (*Wistfully*) Perhaps if I were a free person ...
Haroun (*excitedly*) That's it. He could give you your *freedom* as a reward.

Oh, Marsaina, I'm sure he'll do *that*, and then there'll be nothing to stop us from marrying. Quickly! Let's go and find him.

Haroun and Marsaina exit R

Avarice enters L

Avarice (*snarling*) Once more that slave-girl spoils my plan
To end old Ali's life.
For this, I swear, she has to die.
She'll never be young Haroun's wife.
To Al Raschid will be revealed
The dwelling-place he seeks ...
And all within will perish as
His vengeance fierce, at last, he wreaks.

With a harsh laugh, she exits L *Ali Baba enters* R

Ali (*pleased with himself*) Oh, what a wonderful evening it's going to be tomorrow. Everyone in Cairo will be at my party. Well, everyone of importance. There's no point in inviting *unimportant* people, is there? From now on, all my friends must be rich and famous, as befits my new station in life. I'll make out a list as soon as I get home. (*He sighs happily*) Ah, how satisfying it will be to wear clothes of the finest silks, and eat the same foods as Califs and Sultans.

Raschid enters L, *dressed as a rich merchant*

Ali sees him

Ali Greetings, my friend. (*He salaams with dignity*)

Raschid (*glaring at him*) Out of my way, son of a camel. How dare you speak to Abu Hassan, richest of *all* merchants?

Ali Abu Hassan? (*Scornfully*) Hah. How can *you* be richest of all merchants when *I*, Ali Baba have more wealth than I know what to do with?

Raschid (*sneering*) Indeed? And since when have wealthy merchants walked the streets of Cairo dressed in rags?

Ali Oh, you can sneer, my friend, but I tell you this. Come tomorrow and the name of Ali Baba will be known all over Arabia.

Raschid (*curiously*) And why is that, may I ask?

Ali (*boastfully*) After my brother Kassim is buried, all his wealth will be mine. And when I lead the Caliph's soldiers to the secret hiding place of the Forty Thieves, even greater riches will be showered upon me.

Raschid *You* know their hiding place?

Ali But of course. (*Smugly*) Was it not I who overheard their leader speak the magic word that opened the rocky doors of their treasure cave. And was it not I who recovered my poor brother's body from inside that same place, after the Forty Thieves had cruelly murdered him? (*He preens himself and attempts to look modest*)

Raschid (*aside*) By Allah! I should take my dagger and slit his throat this very moment. But wait ... first I must find out who else knows of our hiding place. (*To Ali, with false warmth*) My dear friend! Let me shake you

Act II, Scene 5

by the hand. (*He does so*) These Forty Thieves have robbed my caravans time and time again. If what you say is true, then I owe you much. But tell me ... who else knows of this secret cave?
Ali (*airily*) Oh, everyone who lives with me. (*Blinking*) Why?
Raschid (*lowering his voice*) Such a secret is best kept quiet. If this information fell into the wrong hands, you could all be in terrible danger.
Ali Yes, but once I tell the Calif tomorrow ...
Raschid Alas. Haven't you heard? The Calif and his soldiers left for Baghdad this morning and will not return until the end of the week.
Ali (*surprised*) Oh. Well, I suppose I can wait a few more days. There's plenty of time, isn't there?
Raschid Aye. Plenty of time for me to be robbed again. Tomorrow afternoon, my latest caravan of camels arrives in Cairo, bearing huge jars of olive oil to sell in the market-place. All day long I've been searching for somewhere to store them in case those accursed Forty Thieves hear about it and rob me once more. But alas, my search has proved fruitless.
Ali (*proudly*) Not at all, Abu Hassan. There's plenty of room in my new stables. You can store your jars of oil there. As soon as your camels arrive, I'll arrange an escort to conduct them to where I live.
Raschid May the Prophet bless you, Ali Baba. You'll never live to regret this.
Ali Oh, well. We merchants must stick together, mustn't we? And as soon as your jars are stored, you must join us in a magnificent feast to celebrate my good fortune. Till tomorrow then.

Ali bows and exits R

Raschid (*triumphantly*) At last. Our search is ended. Tomorrow night shall Ali Baba and his entire household be slaughtered like sheep in their pens. (*He laughs harshly*) But now I must return to the secret cave and instruct my followers on exactly what to do. (*He looks off* R) Farewell, Ali Baba. The next time we meet will be the last.

Raschid laughs again and exits L

Black-out

Scene 5

The Banqueting hall of Ali's new house

A splendid interior befitting an eastern palace. Huge cushions of satin and velvet are lined in a gentle curve all along the back wall, with just enough space for someone to walk behind them. There are no chairs and no other furniture is in evidence. When the scene begins, dancing girls in eastern costume are performing an exotic dance

Dance (Dancers)

At the end of the dance, the dancers hurry off

Cascara enters UL *followed by a despondent-looking Tinbad*

Tinbad Hello. Oh, I aren't half fed up. I've done nothing all afternoon but help unload great big jars of olive oil.
Cascara Oh, stop complaining, can't you? I've had to help as well. Besides, what would you have done if you hadn't been helping? You know you can't go out in the street till that Al Raschid and his gang have been locked away. It'll do you good to do some *real* work for a change.
Tinbad (*indignant*) What do you mean, "real work"?
Cascara Just what I said. You were sitting on that cushion there (*She points*) all morning and not doing a thing, weren't you?
Tinbad (*guiltily*) How do *you* know?
Cascara Because I was standing over there (*She indicates*) watching you.
Tinbad (*defensively*) Well, I was tired out. Don't forget, the night before last I didn't get to bed because I was sewing old Kassim together, and last night I couldn't get to sleep because of all the thunder and lightning.
Cascara Thunder and lightning? (*Annoyed*) Ooh, you stupid great lump. Why didn't you come and waken me up? I've told you before, I can't sleep when it's thundering and lightning. It reminds me of the time when I was a little girl and there was a terrible storm. My poor old mother thought she heard a burglar and had to go all round the house looking for him with nothing but a tiny candle to protect her.
Tinbad And did she find anybody?
Cascara Well, not *downstairs*, but when she got back to the bedroom she saw a pair of men's feet sticking out from underneath the bed.
Tinbad (*wide-eyed*) And was it the burglar?
Cascara No. It was my dad. He thought *he'd* heard the burglar as well. Anyway, never mind about that. There's work to be done before this party starts. You get yourself into the kitchen and mix up some nice drinks for the guests.
Tinbad Here, I've got a smashing new recipe for a cocktail. I found it in the Parish Magazine last month. It's (*He names the local vicar*) 's favourite drink, and comes all the way from America. It's called "Custer's Last Stand".
Cascara "Custer's Last Stand"?
Tinbad Yes. One sip and you'll fall.

Tinbad exits R

Cascara reacts and watches him go

Jiggeri and Hanki enter UL

Jiggeri (*softly*) Anybody home?
Cascara (*turning to see them. Indignantly*) Here, what are *you* doing inside the house? I don't want camel drivers clomping all over me nice clean floor. Go on. Shoo. Shoo. Shoo. (*She ushers them away*)
Hanki No, no, no! You don't understand. We've come here to warn you.
Cascara Warn me? What about?
Jiggeri The jars you were helping to unload a few minutes ago.

Act II, Scene 5   41

Cascara What about them?

Raschid enters DL *in splendid robes*

Raschid Yes. What about them? (*He glares at the two men*)
Hanki Er ... er ... Well ... it's very ... *expensive* oil that's inside them.
Jiggeri (*nodding vigorously*) The best in all Arabia.
Hanki So ... er ... so, you've ... er ... got to make sure that nobody goes anywhere near them in case they accidently break one ...
Jiggeri And spill the oil. (*He gives a weak smile at Raschid*)
Hanki (*nodding*) Spill the oil. (*He looks at Raschid*)
Cascara Oh, you don't have to worry about that. Nobody'll be going into the stables tonight. They'll be too busy enjoying themselves.
Jiggeri Right ... well ... we'd better be off then.
Hanki To ... er ... look after the camels. (*He gives a nervous laugh*)
Raschid (*with menace*) I'll speak to you two later.

Jiggeri and Hanki gulp and exit rapidly UL

(*To Cascara, with exaggerated charm*) Greetings, Madam. Allow me to introduce myself: Abu Hassan, supplier of the finest olive oil in the world and your dinner guest for this evening. (*He smiles broadly*)
Cascara (*simpering*) Ooh, I say ... (*To the audience*) Get a load of this, girls. He's the spitting image of my third husband. He's got so many gold teeth I bet he has to sleep with his head in a safe. (*To Raschid*) I ... er ... I've not seen you around here before, have I?
Raschid (*airily*) It's most unlikely. I was born in Egypt, you see.
Cascara Oh. What part?
Raschid All of me.
Cascara No, no. I mean, whereabouts in Egypt were you born?
Raschid (*realising*) Oh. (*Shrugging*) It's just a small place where all the little rivers run into the Nile. I don't suppose *you've* heard of it.
Cascara Yes I *have*. Everybody's heard of Juveniles. (*She beams*)
Raschid (*grimacing*) Tell me ... Where can I find my dear friend, Ali Baba?
Cascara Oh, I think he's upstairs trying on his new clothes, but if you'd like to come this way, I'll make you a nice cup of tea while you're waiting. (*She simpers and moves* UR)

Raschid follows her and they both exit

Jiggeri and Hanki re-enter

Jiggeri (*worried*) Oh, that's torn it. Fancy *him* coming in just as we were trying to warn her.
Hanki Yes. And now *we're* going to get it in the neck as well.
Jiggeri I know. But we couldn't just stand there and let everybody get killed, could we? It wouldn't be right.
Hanki (*concerned*) What are we going to do now?
Jiggeri We'll have to try again, won't we? I mean, I don't like all this murdering people stuff. I was brought up respectable, I was. My dad was the only one-fingered pickpocket in the whole of Baghdad.
Hanki (*incredulous*) One-fingered pickpocket?

Jiggeri Yes. He used to steal Polo mints.

Hanki (*pushing him*) Idiot. Now listen. There's thirty-eight thieves out there hidden inside those big jars, and as soon as the party starts, they're going to jump out and kill everybody. Now if we want to warn this Ali Baba feller and get out of the city before anybody finds out that *we're* supposed to be part of the gang, we'd better get on with it, hadn't we?

Jiggeri Right. (*He glances off* UR) Here, there's somebody coming now.

They attempt to smarten themselves up

Rhum enters UL

Rhum (*spotting them*) Oh, it's those horrible beggars again. I'll soon get rid of them. (*She marches down to them*) And what, might I ask, are you two doing inside this house?

Hanki (*groaning*) Oh, no. Not you again.

Rhum How dare you protrude into this private establishment? Clear off before I have you *thrown* out.

Jiggeri Eh? You can't throw *us* out, missis. We've come to warn you.

Rhum Warn me?

Hanki Yes. You're all in terrible danger.

Rhum Oh? And why is that, pray?

Jiggeri It's them great big jars of olive oil you've got in the stables. The ones that belong to that feller who calls himself Abu Hassan. They haven't got olive oil in them at all.

Rhum Really? Then what *is* inside them?

Raschid enters UR

Jiggeri (*spotting him*) Er . . . tea.

Rhum Tea?

Hanki (*also spotting Raschid*) With milk and sugar.

Jiggeri That's right. He takes it all over the country with him. Won't go anywhere without it. He loves his cup of tea does our boss.

Song (Jiggeri and Hanki)

At the end of the song, they exit L, *Music Hall style*

Rhum shakes her head in bewilderment and exits DR

Raschid glares L *and moves* DC

Raschid (*grasping his dagger*) If I thought for one minute . . . (*He relaxes*) But no . . . they'd never dare to try and thwart my will. (*He smiles*) The night draws closer. Even now the first stars are in the sky and soon . . . soon . . . shall the wrath of Al Raschid descend upon this miserable household. But before the feast begins, I'll just make sure that everything is as it should be.

He exits L

Ali and Haroun enter UR. *Both are richly dressed*

Haroun (*protesting*) But Father . . .

Act II, Scene 5

Ali For the last time, Haroun, the answer is No. Oh, I know we owe Marsaina a lot, but to give her her freedom is totally out of the question. Where could we find another slave like her? She's intelligent, beautiful, a good seamstress, sings, dances, cooks, keeps the household in order. No wonder my brother Kassim thought so highly of her.

Haroun But don't you understand, Father? I'm in *love* with her.

Ali I'm sure you are, Haroun, but as I told you before, now we're rich, nothing less than a princess will be good enough to be your wife.

Haroun If I can't marry Marsaina, I never want to marry at all.

Ali Nonsense. (*He chuckles*) You'll soon change your mind when you see the beautiful ladies who'll be coming here tonight. Now off you go and prepare yourself. I'm just going to have a word with my special guest Abu Hassan. Cascara tells me he doesn't want salt with his meat, and I can't understand why. I've never heard of such a thing.

He exits L

Marsaina enters DL

Haroun (*going to her*) Oh, Marsaina. It's no use. He wouldn't even listen to me.

Marsaina (*sadly*) I know. I couldn't help overhearing. (*Attempting to brighten up*) But cheer up, Haroun. Even though we can't marry, now you're living here we'll be able to see each other every day. (*She frowns*)

Haroun What's the matter?

Marsaina This merchant your father invited to dinner . . . Abu Hassan.

Haroun What about him?

Marsaina Don't *you* think it's strange that he doesn't want salt with his meat? To share salt is the sign of great friendship in our country. To refuse to share it is the mark of a sworn enemy.

Haroun Oh, I don't think that's the case with Abu Hassan. After all, he's a great merchant and only met my father yesterday.

Marsaina All the same . . . (*She sinks into thought*)

Ali and Raschid enter UR *in deep conversation and cross to exit* UR

Haroun Will you be dancing for us tonight, Marsaina?

Marsaina (*shaking her head*) I'll be far too busy helping in the kitchen. But perhaps after the celebration we could meet for a little while?

Haroun I'll look forward to it with all my heart. Until then . . .

He exits reluctantly R

Cascara enters in a fluster. She is carrying a large jug

Cascara Oh, there you are, Marsaina. The kitchen's in an absolute uproar and I've ruined the entire meal. First of all the chops caught fire, so I had to use the soup to put the flames out, then I slipped in a puddle of fat and dropped the whole lot into the trifle. Now I've got to start all over again. Be a love and pop down to the shop for some more olive oil. (*She hands the jug to Marsaina*)

Marsaina Of course. (*She pauses*) But wait. There are forty jars of olive oil out in the stables. I'm sure no-one would mind if we borrowed a small amount.

Cascara Oh, what a good idea. We can always pay him for it later.

Marsaina exits L

(*To audience*) Ooh, it's murder back there, you know. You can't move in that kitchen. Reminds me of the time I worked in the restaurant down the road. Oooh, what a posh place *that* was. I'll tell you this much. It was so posh, they used to make the gravy in fifty different colours to match the clothes the customers wore. Here, and what a snooty lot *they* were, I can tell you. Even the bags under their eyes were made of crocodile skin. I remember *one* customer coming in and asking me "What have you got today?" so I told him," Stewed kidneys, boiled tongue, calves brains, ox liver and pigs feet". Well, he looked me up and down and said "Don't tell me *your* problems, Missis. Give me some roast beef and go see a doctor." But the *complaints* you get from some folk. You wouldn't believe it. There was one woman complained she'd got a bar of soap in her Shepherd's Pie. I said, "I know you have. It's to wash the food down." Then there was the feller who moaned about his chicken. "It's only got one leg," he said. "I know," I told him. "It must have been in a fight." He said, "Well take it back and bring me the winner." But honestly . . .

Marsaina enters breathlessly

Marsaina Cascara. Cascara. We're all in great danger.

Cascara (*startled*) Eh? We haven't got (*She names famous comedian or double-act*) in, writing all the jokes down, have we?

Marsaina No, no. It's even more serious than that. The jars out there. Only two of them contain olive oil. The rest of them have men hidden inside.

Cascara Men in jars? Well *there's* a novelty. Shall we order a dozen between us?

Marsaina (*desperately*) You don't understand, Cascara. Forty jars. A man who refuses to share salt with Ali Baba. Abu Hassan must be Al Raschid in disguise, and his Forty Thieves are inside those jars waiting to spring out and murder us all.

Cascara (*startled*) Oooh, I say. Are you sure?

Marsaina I accidently bumped against one of the jars as I went in and a man's voice asked if it were time. I replied, "Not yet", and went on to the next. There was a man inside that, too. There are men inside all of them but two.

Cascara (*stricken*) Oh, whatever are we going to do? I'm too young to die.

Marsaina I have an idea. Take the two jars of *real* oil into the kitchen and set them over the fire to heat. Then as soon as it's bubbling, we must pour it into the jars containing the robbers and boil them alive. It's the only way to save ourselves.

Cascara And what about this Al Raschid character? What are we going to do about him?

Marsaina Leave that to me. Tonight I *shall* dance at the feast.

She hurries off UR

Act II, Scene 5

Cascara Ooh, I'd better get Tinbad to lend me a hand. I'll never be able to shift them things on my own.

Cascara exits UR

Cascara (*off*) Tinbad, Tinbad.

Avarice enters DL

Avarice By all I hold accurs*ed* ... now
That whey-faced, simp'ring slave
Has learned the Robbers' secret and
Will send them all to oily grave.
But though she does her worst, I swear
By my eternal name ...
That Al Raschid will beat her yet
And win this little game.

Morgana enters DR

Morgana Beware, dear sister Avarice,
And hear this promise true.
From now on, should you interfere,
Then *I* shall put an end to *you*

She mimes drawing out a strand

Just like the mortals here on earth,
Your fate is in my hand.

She grasps each end of the strand

Should something evil harm that girl
I vow I'll *snap* this strand.
Avarice (*aghast*) You wouldn't dare.
Morgana Just tempt me. In the twinkling of an eye,
You'd shrink and shrivel into dust,
And that same instant, die.
Avarice (*bitterly*) A curse on you, Morgana.
This threat is quite unfair.
You leave me no alternative
But to depart on desert air. (*She begins to move off, then pauses*)
But mark my words ... although I'm gone
Raschid will win the day.
'Gainst him, Marsaina stands *no* chance.
And now, my friend, good-day.

Avarice gives a mocking curtsy and with a cackle of evil laughter exits L

Morgana (*smiling*) We'll see. The tangled threads of Fate
On Fortune's wheel now spin.
Come forth, the players of this game
And may the best one win.

Morgana exits proudly R

Ali, Raschid, Haroun and Rhum enter, in seemingly friendly conversation. Guests and servants also enter L *and* R. *The four principals seat themselves on the cushions with Raschid* L, *Ali next to him, Haroun, then Rhum* R. *Others sit cross-legged at the sides of the room. Servants stand at various points, each holding a basket of fruit, or feather fans on long poles. The scene should look as rich and colourful as possible*

Ali May the blessing of Allah be on all of us. Let the entertainment begin.

There is the jangle of tambourines, and six dancing girls appear. They circle the dancing area, shaking the tambourines and swirling around, before dropping to one knee and striking a pose

Marsaina enters dressed as a dancing girl, and holding two daggers

Haroun (*surprised*) Marsaina!

Without speaking, Marsaina begins her dance

Dance (Marsaina)

During the course of the dance, Marsaina pretends to menace various people with her daggers. All encourage her with smiles and pretended alarm. Finally, as the music rises to a climax, she moves to Raschid's side and with a cry, plunges one of the daggers into his heart. Everyone reacts as Raschid dies. Marsaina at once drops her daggers as they all scramble to their feet

Ali What have you *done*? Guards! Guards! Arrest this woman at once.

Marsaina Wait. My lord. First look inside the robes of this "honest" merchant.

Ali bends over Raschid, and fumbling under his robe produces Raschid's own dagger. There is a gasp from everyone

Ali (*confused*) I don't understand.

Marsaina This Abu Hassan was no merchant, my lord Ali, but Al Raschid, leader of the Forty Thieves. Here tonight to kill not only you, but everyone in your household.

There is shocked reaction from all

Rhum Oh, my goodness. But if this is true, what about the others? Where are *they*? (*She looks round fearfully*)

Cascara and Tinbad enter L

Cascara Oh, you don't have to worry about *them* any more. We covered 'em in onions and deep fried the lot of 'em.

Ali (*overcome*) Oh, Marsaina. You've saved us once more. However can I repay you?

Tinbad Well, there is *one* way. Give her her freedom.

Ali Freedom? (*To Audience*) Do *you* think I should? (*Audience reaction*) Very well then ... I will. From this moment on, Marsaina is free.

Act II, Scene 6

All react with delight

Haroun Then in that case, there can be no objection to my marrying her, Father.

Ali None whatsoever, my son. And may you both be eternally happy.

Marsaina and Haroun hurry to each other

(*Indicating Raschid's body*) Remove this vile carcass from our sight.

The body is carried out

Haroun   And now let happiness hold sway,
                  As we celebrate our Wedding Day.

There is a cheer from all

                  Song 16 (Full Company)

Black-out

Scene 6

A corridor

Jiggeri and Hanki enter. They speak to the audience

Jiggeri Well, here we are again. Out of a job and not even a penny to buy a cup of tea with.

Hanki Still, that's better than being boiled in oil like all the others, isn't it? Anyway, it serves them right. Doesn't it, kids?

Jiggeri Yes. And even *we've* turned over a new leaf. We're not going to be thieves any more. We're going to do a job where you can earn some *real* money. We're going to be pop singers.

Hanki That's right. But before we go see the feller in the recording studio, we've got to get a backing group. You know, somebody to sing along *with* us. *You* don't know anybody that could do that, do you?

Jiggeri Here, I've had an idea. (*To Hanki*) Maybe *they* could do it? There's plenty of 'em out there.

Hanki Hey, you're right. (*To the audience*) Do you think you could?

Audience reaction

    Right. We'll give it a go, then.

                Song Sheet (Jiggeri, Hanki and Audience)

Lights fade rapidly at the end of the song

   Jiggeri and Hanki exit L *and* R

Scene 7

The banqueting hall again

As before, but all the cushions, etc. have been removed. Full lighting. The walk-down now begins

>Babes
>Dancers
>Chorus
>Achmed
>Morgana and Avarice
>Kassim and Rhum
>Jiggeri and Hanki
>Al Raschid
>Cascara and Tinbad
>Ali Baba
>Haroun and Marsaina

If required, there can be a reprise of one of the songs used in the show

Haroun	Our show, alas, is ended. It's time to say goodnight.
Marsaina	We hope, for just an hour or so, we've filled you with delight.
Cascara	A bit of eastern promise. (*She simpers*)
Tinbad	Which no trace of sadness leaves.
Ali	Sweet dreams to each and all of you.
All	From Ali Baba and the Forty Thieves.

The reprise is sung once more

>*Finale*
>
>Curtain

FURNITURE AND PROPERTY LIST

ACT I

Scene 1

On stage: Stalls
Palm-trees

Personal: **Tinbad:** sheet of paper
Ali Baba: bundle of sticks
Marsaina: basket of food
Raschid: dagger
Jiggeri: small bottle

Scene 2

On stage: Seven palm-trees

Personal: **Haroun:** basket

Scene 3

On stage: Cliff boulders
Stunted trees
Magic cave

Off stage: Small sack of gold **(Ali Baba)**

Personal: **Thieves:** weapons, sacks
Hanki: blindfold
Jiggeri: blindfold

Scene 4

Personal: **Ali Baba:** small sack of gold

Scene 5

On stage: Row of shabby hovels, middle one with practical door

ACT II

Scene 1

On stage: Stalls
Palm-trees

Personal: **Raschid:** dagger
Thieves: daggers

Scene 2

On stage: Tumbledown shops
Personal: **Tinbad:** teddy-bear, blindfold

Scene 3

On stage: Stalls
Palm-trees
Personal: **Tinbad:** teddy-bear, small bag of gold
Raschid: large handkerchief, dagger

Scene 4

On stage: Nil

Scene 5

On stage: Velvet and satin cushions
Off stage: Two daggers **(Marsaina)**
Personal: **Cascara:** jug
Raschid: dagger

Scene 6

On stage: Nil

Scene 7

On stage: Nil

LIGHTING PLOT

ACT I, SCENE 1

To open: Full, general lighting

Cue 1   **Haroun:** "Coming, Father".   (Page 6)
Lights flicker

ACT I, SCENE 2

To open: Evening sunlight

Cue 2   **Avarice** exits   (Page 13)

Cue 3   Storm builds to a climax   (Page 13)
Black-out
Lights flicker

ACT I, SCENE 3

To open: Dawn light

Cue 4   **Sand spirits** exit   (Page 13)
Bring up Lights

Cue 5   **Ali Baba** enters magic cave   (Page 17)
Dim Lights

Cue 6   **Avarice** exits   (Page 17)
Bring up Lights

Cue 7   **Ali Baba** exits   (Page 17)
Fade to Black-out

ACT I, SCENE 4

To open: Full, general lighting

Cue 8   **Cascara** exits   (Page 20)
Fade to Black-out

ACT I, SCENE 5

To open: Full, general lighting

No cues

ACT II, SCENE 1

To open: Full, general lighting

Cue 9	**Cascara** and **Tinbad** exit *Lights flicker*	(Page 27)
Cue 10	**Morgana:** "To bring happy, peaceful end". *Lights fade to sunset*	(Page 28)
Cue 11	**Raschid** exits *Lights fade to Black-out*	(Page 30)

ACT II, SCENE 2

To open: Gloomy, shadowy lighting

Cue 12	**Hanki** and **Jiggeri** exit *Lights fade to Black-out*	(Page 31)

ACT II, SCENE 3

To open: Dawn light

Cue 13	At end of Song 14 *Black-out*	(Page 37)

ACT II, SCENE 4

To open: Full, general lighting

Cue 14	**Raschid** exits *Black-out*	(Page 39)

ACT II, SCENE 5

To open: Full, general lighting

Cue 15	**Cascara:** "Tinbad! Tinbad!" *Lights flicker*	(Page 45)
Cue 16	**Morgana** exits *Bring up Lights*	(Page 46)
Cue 17	At end of Song 16 *Black-out*	(Page 47)

ACT II, SCENE 6

To open: Full, general lighting

Cue 18	At the end of song *Lights fade to Black-out*	(Page 47)

ACT II, SCENE 7

To open: Full, general lighting

No cues

EFFECTS PLOT

ACT I

Cue 1	**Haroun:** "Coming, Father". *Swirling vapour*	(Page 6)
Cue 2	**Avarice** exits *Wind, effects, storm*	(Page 13)
Cue 3	**Raschid** (firmly): "Open, Sesame". *Great grinding of rock*	(Page 16)
Cue 4	**Raschid** (loudly): "Close, Sesame". *Loud grating as boulder closes*	(Page 16)
Cue 5	**Ali** (loudly): "Open, Sesame". *Repeat Cue 3*	(Page 17)
Cue 6	**Ali** (loudly): "Close, Sesame". *Repeat Cue 4*	(Page 17)

ACT II

No cues

MADE AND PRINTED IN GREAT BRITAIN BY
LATIMER TREND & COMPANY LTD PLYMOUTH
MADE IN ENGLAND